Insights to Help You Survive the Peaks and Valleys

Can You Stand to Be Blessed?

BISHOP T.D. JAKES

Treasure House
An Imprint of
Destiny Image® Publishers, Inc.
P.O. Box 310, Shippensburg, PA 17257-0310

*"For where your treasure is,
there will your heart be also"* Matthew 6:21.

ISBN 10: 0-7684-2619-7
ISBN 13: 978-0-7684-2619-9

Previously Published as ISBN 1-56043-801-0 and 0-7684-3042-9

For Worldwide Distribution
Printed in the U.S.A.

This book and all other Destiny Image, Revival Press, Mercy-Place, Fresh Bread, Destiny Image Fiction, and Treasure House books are available at Christian bookstores and distributors worldwide.

For a U.S. bookstore nearest you, call 1-800-722-6774.
Or reach us on the Internet: www.destinyimage.com.

4 5 6 7 8 9 10 11 / 11 10 09 08

Insights to Help You Survive the Peaks and Valleys

DEDICATION

I dedicate this book to Dr. Sherman S. Watkins, whose wisdom and unfailing love has stimulated the seeds of greatness in my life. I deeply appreciate that wisdom; it caused me to realize in the early stages of my ministry that blessings cannot be computed or counted, for the true blessings of life are the treasures hidden in the reservoirs of the human heart. Because of his confidence and counsel, I "can stand to be blessed."

CONTENTS

Chapter 1   The Transformers 9

Chapter 2   Don't Count Me Out! 21

Chapter 3   Delayed But Not Denied 31

Chapter 4   Refiner's Fire 43

Chapter 5   I Am Come in My Father's Name 55

Chapter 6   Romancing a Stone? 67

Chapter 7   Offspring, Oddities, and Obstacles 85

Chapter 8   Living on the Left Side of God 99

Chapter 9   A Survival Course for Small Beginnings. . 115

Chapter 10   Can You Stand to Be Blessed? 125

Chapter 11   Return to Sender 141

Chapter 12   It's Just Your Time 159

Chapter 1

THE TRANSFORMERS

But as many as received Him, to them gave He power to become the sons of God, even to them that believe on His name (John 1:12).

I pray that we as Christians never lose our conviction that God does change lives. We must protect this message. Our God enables us to make the radical changes necessary for fulfilling our purposes and responsibilities. Like the caterpillar that eats and sleeps its way into change, the process occurs gradually, but nonetheless powerfully. Many people who will rock this world are sleeping in the cocoon of obscurity, waiting for their change to come. The Scriptures declare, "...it is high time to awake out of sleep: for now is our salvation nearer than when we believed" (Rom. 13:11).

A memory of my twin sons playing on the floor when they were children tailors the continuity of this text for me. They were playing with a truck, contributing all the sounds of grinding gears and roaring engines. I didn't pay much attention as I began unwinding from the day's stresses and challenges. Distractedly, I glanced down at the floor and noticed that the boys were now running an airplane down an imaginary runway. I asked, "What happened to the truck you were playing with?" They explained, "Daddy, this is a transformer!" I then inquired, "What is a transformer?" Their answer brought me into the Presence of the Lord. They said, "It can be transformed from what it was before into whatever we want it to be!"

Suddenly I realized that God had made the first transformer! He created man from dust. He created him in such a way that, if need be, He could pull a woman out of him without ever having to reach back into the dust. Out of one creative act God transformed the man into a marriage. Then He transformed the marriage into a family, the family into a society, etc. God never had to reach into the ground again because the power to transform was intrinsically placed into man. All types of potential were locked into our spirits before birth. For the Christian, transformation at its optimum is the outworking of the internal. God placed certain things in us that must come out. We house the prophetic power of God. Every word of our personal prophetic destiny is inside us. He has ordained us to be!

> *Before I formed thee in the belly I knew thee; and before thou camest forth out of the womb I sanctified thee, and I ordained thee a prophet unto the nations* (Jeremiah 1:5).

Only when we are weary from trying to unlock our own resources do we come to the Lord, receive Him, and allow Him to release in us the power to become whatever we need to be. Actually, isn't that what we want to know—our purpose? Then we can use the power to become who we really are. Life has chiseled many of us into mere fragments of who we were meant to be. To all who receive Him, Christ gives the power to slip out of who they were forced into being so they can transform into the individual they each were created to be.

Salvation as it relates to destiny is the God-given power to become what God has eternally decreed you were before. "Before what?" you ask; before the foundation of the world. What Christians so often refer to as grace truly is God's divine enablement to accomplish predestined purpose. When the Lord says to Paul, "My grace is sufficient for thee..." (2 Cor. 12:9), He is simply stating that His power is not intimidated by your circumstances. You are empowered by God to reach and accomplish goals that transcend human limitations! It is important that each and every vessel God uses realize that they were able to accomplish what others could not only because God gave them the grace to do so. Problems are not really problems to a person who has the grace to serve in a particular area.

How many times have people walked up to me and said, "I don't see how you can stand this or that." If God has given us the grace to operate in a certain situation, those things do not affect us as they would someone else who does not have the grace to function in that area. Therefore, it is important that we not imitate other people. Assuming that we may be equally talented, we still may not be equally graced. Remember, God always empowers whomever He employs. Ultimately, we must realize that the excellency of our gifts are of God and not of us. He doesn't need nearly as much of our contributions as we think He does. So it is God who works out the internal destinies of men. He gives us the power to become who we are eternally and internally.

> *Wherefore, my beloved, as ye have always obeyed, not as in my presence only, but now much more in my absence, work out your own salvation with fear and trembling. For it is God which worketh in you both to will and to do of His good pleasure* (Philippians 2:12-13).

Today in the Body of Christ a great deal of emphasis is placed on the process of mentoring. The concept of mentoring is both scriptural and effective; however, as we often do, many of us have gone to extremes. Instead of teaching young men to pursue God, the ultimate Rabbi, they are running amuck looking for a man to pour into them. All men are not mentored as Joshua was—under the firm hand of a strong leader. Some, like Moses, are prepared by the workings of the manifold wisdom of God. This latter group receive mentoring through the carefully orchestrated circumstances that God ordains to accomplish an end result. Regardless of which describes your ascent to greatness, it is still God who "worketh in you both to will and to do." When you understand this, you appreciate the men or the methods God used, but ultimately praise the God whose masterful ability to conduct has crescendoed in the finished product of a man or woman of God.

> *And the Lord said unto Moses, Gather unto Me seventy men of the elders of Israel, whom thou knowest to be the elders of the people, and officers over them; and*

bring them unto the tabernacle of the congregation, that they may stand there with thee (Numbers 11:16).

In keeping with this mentoring concept, let's consider Moses' instructions when asked to consecrate elders in Israel. I found it interesting that God told Moses to gather unto Him men whom he knew were elders. God says, "I want you to separate men to be elders who are elders." You can only ordain a man to be what he already is. The insight we need to succeed is the discernment of who is among us. Woe unto the man who is placed into what he is not. Moses was to bring these men into a full circle. In other words, they were to be led into what they already were. Perhaps this will further clarify my point: When the prodigal son was in the "hog pen," it was said, "And when he came to himself..." (Lk. 15:17). We are fulfilled only when we are led into being who we were predestined to be. Real success is coming to ourselves.

The thing that gives a man power to arise above his circumstances is his coming to himself. You feel fulfilled when you achieve a sense of belonging through your job, family, or ministry. Have you ever met anyone who left you with a feeling of familiarity—almost as if you had known the person? A sense of bonding comes out of similarities. Likewise, there are certain jobs or ministries that feel comfortable, even if they are tasks you have never done before. If you are discerning, you can feel a sense of belonging in certain situations. However, weary are the legs of a traveler who cannot find his way home. Spiritual wanderings plague the lives of many people who wrestle with discontentment. May God grant you success in finding your way to a sense of wholeness and completion.

Change is a gift from God. It is given to the person who finds himself too far removed from what he feels destiny has ordained for him. There is nothing wrong with being wrong—but there is something wrong with not making the necessary adjustments to get things right! Even within the Christian community, some do not believe in God's ability to change the human heart. This unbelief in God's ability to change causes people to judge others on the basis of their past. Dead issues are periodically revived in the mouths of gossips. Still, the Lord progressively regenerates the mind of His children. Don't assume that real change occurs without struggle and prayer. However, change can be achieved.

> *God exalted Him to His own right hand as Prince and Savior that He might give repentance and forgiveness of sins to Israel* (Acts 5:31 NIV).

The Bible calls change *repentance*. Repentance is God's gift to a struggling heart who wants to find himself. The Lord wants to bring you to a place of safety and shelter. Without the Holy Spirit's help you can search and search and still not find repentance. The Lord will show the place of repentance only to those who hunger and thirst after righteousness. One moment with the Spirit of God can lead you into a place of renewal that, on your own, you would not find or enjoy. I believe it was this kind of grace that made John Newton record, "It was grace that taught my heart to fear and grace my fears relieved. How precious did that grace appear the hour I first believed"

("Amazing Grace," early American melody). When God gives you the grace to make changes that you know you couldn't do with your own strength, it becomes precious to you.

> For ye know how that afterward, when he would have inherited the blessing, he was rejected: for he found no place of repentance, though he sought it carefully with tears (Hebrews 12:17).

Brother Esau sought for the place of repentance and could not secure it. To be transformed is to be changed. If you are not moving into your divine purpose, you desperately need to repent. "Repent" has a strong negative connotation for the person indoctrinated to believe that repentance is a fearful and dangerous action. It is not dangerous. Repentance is the prerequisite of revival. There cannot be revival without prayerful repentance. John the Baptist taught Israel, "Repent ye: for the kingdom of heaven is at hand" (Mt. 3:2). If God wants you to change, it is because He wants you to be prepared for what He desires to do next in your life. Get ready; the best is yet to come.

> For whom He did foreknow, He also did predestinate to be conformed to the image of His Son, that He might be the firstborn among many brethren (Romans 8:29).

> And be not conformed to this world: but be ye transformed by the renewing of your mind, that ye may prove what is that good, and acceptable, and perfect, will of God (Romans 12:2).

Now let's deal with some real issues! The word *conformed* in Romans 8:29 is *summorphoo* (James Strong, *The*

Exhaustive Concordance of the Bible [Peabody, MA: Hendrickson Publishers, n.d.], #G4832), which means "to be fashioned like or shaped into the image or the picture" of—in this case—Christ. God has predestined you to shape up into a picture of Christ in the earth. Christ is the firstborn of a huge family of siblings who all bear a striking resemblance to their Father. The shaping of a will, however, requires a visit to the garden of Gethsemane. *Gethsemane* literally means "oil press" (Strong's #G1068). God presses the oil of His anointing out of your life through adversity. When you forsake your will in order to be shaped into a clearer picture of Christ, you will see little drops of oil coming out in your walk and work for God. In short, He predestined the pressing in your life that produces the oil. As you are pressed, you gradually conform to the image of your predestined purpose.

In Romans 12:2 we are instructed not to be conformed to this world. Literally, it says we are not to be conformed to the same pattern of this world. The text warns us against submitting to the dictates of the world. We are to avoid using those standards as a pattern for our progress. On a deeper level God is saying, "Do not use the same pattern of the world to measure success or to establish character and values." The term *world* in Greek is *aion* (Strong's #G165), which refers to ages. Together these words tell us, "Do not allow the pattern of the times you are in to become the pattern that shapes your inward person."

At this point I can almost hear someone saying, "How do you respond to the preexisting circumstances and conditions that have greatly affected you?" Or, "I am already shaped into something less than what God would want me to be because of the times in which I live or the circumstances in which I grew up." I am glad you asked these things. You see, every aspect of your being that has already been conformed to this age must be transformed! The prefix *trans* implies movement, as in the words *transport, translate, transact, transition,* etc. In this light, *transform* would imply moving the form. On a deeper level it means moving from one form into another, as in the tadpole that is transformed into the frog and the caterpillar into the butterfly. No matter what has misfigured you, in God is the power to be transformed.

Many individuals in the Body of Christ are persevering without progressing. They wrestle with areas that have been conformed to the world instead of transformed. This is particularly true of we Pentecostals who often emphasize the gifts of the Spirit and exciting services. It is imperative that, while we keep our mode of expression, we understand that transformation doesn't come from inspiration! Many times preachers sit down after ministering a very inspiring sermon feeling that they accomplished more than they actually did. Transformation takes place in the mind.

The Bible teaches that we are to be renewed by the transforming of our minds (see Rom. 12:2; Eph. 4:23). Only the Holy Spirit knows how to renew the mind. The struggle we have inside us is with our self-perception. Generally our perception of ourselves is affected by those around us. Our early opinion of ourselves is deeply affected by the opinions of the authoritative figures in our formative years. If our parents tend to neglect or ignore us, it tears at our self-worth. Eventually, though, we mature to the degree where we can walk in the light of our own self-image, without its being diluted by the contributions of others.

When we experience the new birth, we again go back to the formative years of being deeply impressionable. It's important to be discerning in who we allow to influence us in the early years. Whenever we become intimate with someone, the first thing we should want to know is, "Who do you say that I am?" Our basic need is to be understood by the inner circle of people with whom we walk. However, we must be ready to abort negative, destructive information that doesn't bring us into an accelerated awareness of inner realities and strengths. Jesus was able to ask Peter, "Who do you say that I am?" because He already knew the answer! (See Matthew 16:15.) To ask someone to define you without first knowing the answer within yourself is dangerous. When we ask that kind of question, without an inner awareness, we open the door for manipulation. In short, Jesus knew who He was.

The Lord wants to help you realize who you are and what you are graced to do. When you understand that He is the only One who really knows you, then you pursue Him with fierceness and determination. Pursue Him! Listen to what Paul shares at the meeting on Mars' Hill.

> *And hath made of one blood all nations of men for to dwell on all the face of the earth, and hath determined the times before appointed, and the bounds of their habitation; that they should seek the Lord, if haply they*

might feel after Him, and find Him, though He be not far from every one of us: for in Him we live, and move, and have our being; as certain also of your own poets have said, For we are also His offspring (Acts 17:26-28).

The basic message of this passage is that God has set the bounds on our habitations. He knows who we are and how we are to attain. This knowledge, locked up in the counsel of God's omniscience, is the basis of our pursuit, and it is the release of that knowledge that brings immediate transformation. He knows the hope or the goal of our calling. He is not far removed from us; He reveals Himself to people who seek Him. The finders are the seekers. The door is opened only to the knockers and the gifts are given to the askers! (See Luke 11:9.) Initiation is our responsibility. Whosoever hungers and thirsts shall be filled. Remember, in every crisis He is never far from the seeker!

Transforming truths are brought forth through the birth canal of our diligence in seeking His face. It is while you are in His presence that He utters omniscient insights into your individual purpose and course. Jesus told a woman who had been wrestling with a crippling condition for 18 years that she was not really bound—that in fact she was loosed! Immediately she was transformed by the renewing of her mind. (See Luke 13:11-13.) It is no wonder David said, "In Thy presence is fulness of joy" (Ps. 16:11b). The answer is in the Presence—the Presence of God, not man! There is a renewing word that will change your mind about your circumstance. Just when the enemy thinks he has you, transform before his very eyes!

No matter who left his impression upon you, God's Word prevails! The obstacles of past scars can be overcome by present truths. Your deliverance will not start in your circumstances; it will always evolve out of your mentality. As the Word of God waxes greater, the will of men becomes weaker. Paul said in Ephesians 5:26 that Jesus cleanses by the "washing of water by the word." So turn the faucet on high and ease your mind down into the sudsy warm water of profound truth. Gently wash away every limitation and residue of past obstacles and gradually, luxuriously, transform into the refreshed, renewed person you were created to become. Whenever someone tells you what you can't do or be, or what you can't get or attain, then tell them, "I can do all things through Christ who strengthens me! I am a transformer!"

Chapter 2

Don't Count Me Out!

Jesus seldom attended funerals. When He did, it was to arrest death and stop the ceremony. If you are planning an elaborate ceremony to celebrate your nonparticipation in the plan of God, I must warn you that God doesn't hang around funerals. Sometimes Christians become frustrated and withdraw from activity on the basis of personal struggles. They think it's all over, but God says not so! The best is yet to come. The Lord doesn't like pity parties, and those who have them are shocked to find that although He is invited, He seldom attends. Many morbid mourners will come to sit with you as you weep over your dear departed dreams. But if you want the Lord to come, you mustn't tell Him that you aren't planning to get up.

If you ever get around people who have accomplished much, they will tell you that those accomplishments didn't come without price. Generally that cost is much more expensive than you normally want to pay. Still, the cost of total transformation means different things to different people. When you arrive at your destination, don't be surprised that some people will assume everything you achieved came without price. The real price of success lies within the need to persevere. The trophy is never given to someone who does not complete the task. Setbacks are just setups for God to show what He is able to do. Funerals are for people who have accepted the thought that everything is over. Don't do that; instead tell the enemy, "I am not dead yet."

> *For a just man falleth seven times, and riseth up again: but the wicked shall fall into mischief* (Proverbs 24:16).

The whole theme of Christianity is one of rising again. However, you can't rise until you fall. Now that doesn't mean you should fall into sin. It means you should allow the resurrecting power of the Holy Ghost to operate in your life regardless of whether you have fallen into sin, discouragement, apathy, or fear. There are obstacles that can trip you as you escalate toward productivity. But it doesn't matter what tripped you; it matters that you rise up. People who never experience these things generally are people who don't do anything. There is a certain safety in being dormant. Nothing is won, but nothing is lost. I would rather walk on the water with Jesus. I would rather nearly drown and have to be saved than play it safe and never experience the miraculous.

When the AIDS epidemic hit this country, pandemonium erupted. Terror caused many people, Christians as well as non-Christians, to react out of ignorance and intimidation. The media continually presented the sickness as it attacked many individuals in highly visible positions. In listening to the discussions on TV and elsewhere, the primary concern didn't seem to be for the victim. People were whispering, wanting to know how it was contracted. I told the church I pastor that it was absolutely absurd to concern themselves with how anybody contracted AIDS. The issue is that they have it, and what are we going to do to help? It is not as though the disease is any less vicious to someone whom we approve of or exonerate. It has the same effect. Many are the methods by which we can contract it, but somewhere there will be but one cure.

In that same sense, regardless of what causes us to fall, what matters is that we get up! The enemy wants to lull us into a state of acceptance whereby we consider ourselves unable to alter the circumstances that limit us. However, the just man is successful because he continues to get up. The Holy Spirit challenges us to stand in the midst of contrary winds, and if we stumble to our knees, to grasp the hand of God's grace and arise.

If we intend to accomplish anything, we must react to adversity like yeast. Once yeast is thoroughly stirred into the dough, it cannot be detected. Although it is invisible, it is highly effective. When the heat is on, it will rise. The warmer the circumstance, the greater the reaction. Likewise, God sets us in warm, uncomfortable places so we can rise. Consider Israel in Egypt. The more the enemy afflicted them, the more the Israelites grew. Sometimes the worst times in our lives do more to strengthen us than all our mountaintop experiences. The power of God reacts to struggle and stress. Isn't that what God meant when He told Paul, "...My strength is made perfect in weakness" (2 Cor. 12:9a)?

Several years ago a young man walked up to me and said, "I am getting ready to pioneer a church. Do you have any advice for me?" In fact, he asked, "If you could sum up in one word what it takes to be effective in ministry, what would that word be?" I thought about it a moment, then responded, "Relentless!" You must be a person who is relentless—always abounding in the work of the Lord. If you give up easily, there is no need for you to attempt to accomplish much for God. *Relentless* is a word I use to describe people who will not take no for an answer! They try things one way, and if that doesn't work, they try it another way. But they don't give up. You who are about to break beneath the stress of intense struggles, be relentless! Do not quit!

A terrible thing happens to people who give up too easily. It is called *regret*. It is the nagging, gnawing feeling that says, "If I had tried harder, I could have succeeded." When counseling married couples, I always encourage them to be sure they have done everything within their power to build a successful marriage. It is terrible to lay down at night thinking, "I wonder what would have happened if I had tried this or that." Granted, we all experience some degree of failure. That is how we learn and grow. If a baby had to learn how to walk without falling, he would never learn. A baby learns as much from falling on his bottom as he does from his first wobbly steps. The problem isn't failure; it is when we fail and question if it was our lack of commitment that allowed us to forfeit an opportunity to turn the test into a triumph! We can never be sure of the answer unless we rally our talents, muster our courage, and focus our strength to achieve a goal. If we don't have the passion to be relentless, then we should leave it alone.

You would be surprised to know how many people there are who never focus on a goal. They do several things haphazardly without examining how forceful they can be when they totally commit themselves to a cause. The difference between the masterful and the mediocre is often a focused effort. On the other hand, mediocrity is masterful to persons of limited resources and abilities. So in reality, true success is relative to ability. What is a miraculous occurrence for one person can be nothing of consequence to another. A person's goal must be set on the basis of his ability to cultivate talents and his agility in provoking a change. I often wonder how far my best work is in front of me. I am convinced that I have not fully developed my giftings. But, I am committed to the cause of being. "Being what?" you ask. I am committed to being all that I was intended and predestined to be for the Lord, for my family, and for myself. How about you—have you decided to roll up your sleeves and go to work? Remember, effort is the bridge between mediocrity and masterful accomplishment!

Multiple talents can also be a source of confusion. People who are effective at only one thing have little to decide. At this point let me distinguish between talent and purpose. You may have within you a multiplicity of talent. But if the Holy Spirit gives no direction in that area, it will not be effective. Are you called to the area in which you feel talented? On the other hand, consider this verse: "And we know that all things work together for good to them that love God, to them who are the called according to His purpose" (Rom. 8:28). So then you are called according to His purpose and not your talents. You should have a sense of purpose in your ministry and not just talent.

I realize that this idea is highly controversial; however, if you are only talented, you may feel comfortable taking your talents into a secular arena. Talent, like justice, is blind; it will seek all opportunities the same. But when you are cognizant of divine purpose, there are some things you will not do because they would defeat the purpose of God in your life! For instance, if it is your purpose to bless the Body of Christ in song or ministry, though you may be talented enough to aspire to some secular platform of excellence, if you are cognizant of your purpose, you will do what you are called to do. Being called according to purpose enables you to focus on the development of your talent as it relates to your purpose!

Whenever we bring our efforts into alignment with His purpose, we automatically are blessed. Second Timothy 2:4-5 says, "No man that warreth entangleth himself with the affairs of this life; that he may please him who hath chosen him to be a soldier. And if a man also strive for masteries, yet is he not crowned, except he strive lawfully." In order to strive lawfully, our efforts must be tailored after the pattern of divine purpose. Everyone is already blessed. We often spend hours in prayer trying to convince God that He should bless what we are trying to accomplish. What we need to do is spend hours in prayer for God to reveal His purpose. When we do what God has ordained to be done, we are blessed because God's plan is already blessed.

Perhaps you have known times of frustration. Most of us at one time or another have found ourselves wrestling to birth an idea that was conceived in the womb of the human mind as opposed to the divine. For myself, I learned that God will not be manipulated. If He said it, that settles it. No amount of praying through parched lips and tear-stained eyes will cause God to avert what He knows is best for you. I know so well how it feels to find yourself sitting on the side of the bed when you should have been sleeping. I have struggled in the process of anguished surrender. James Taylor had a secular song entitled, "Help Me Make It Through the Night." Those night experiences come to everyone. Those turbulent, boisterous winds of indecisiveness blow severely against the human constitution. The Psalmist also shares his testimony:

> *O Lord, how many are my foes! How many rise up against me! Many are saying of me, "God will not deliver him." Selah. But You are a shield around me, O Lord; You bestow glory on me and lift up my head. To the Lord I cry aloud, and He answers me from His holy hill. Selah* (Psalm 3:1-4 NIV).

> *I laid me down and slept; I awaked; for the Lord sustained me* (Psalm 3:5).

David declares that it is the Lord who sustains you in the perilous times of inner struggle and warfare. It is the precious peace of God that eases your tension when you are trying to make decisions in the face of criticism and cynicism. When you realize that some people do not want you to be successful, the pressure mounts drastically. Many have said, "God will not deliver him." However, many saying it still doesn't make it true. I believe that the safest place in the whole world is in the will of God. If you align your plan with His purpose, success is imminent! On the other hand, if I have not been as successful as I would like to be, then seeking the purpose of God inevitably enriches my resources and makes the impossible attainable. If the storm comes and I know I am in the will of God, then little else matters.

I remember when my wife and I were raising two children (now we have four). Times were tough and money was scarce. I am not the kind of husband who doesn't care about the provisions of the Lord in his house. So many were the nights that I languished over the needs in our home. Tossing and turning, praying and worrying—I wasn't sure we were going to survive the struggle. During these times satan always shows you images of yourself and your children wrapped up in dirty quilts, nestled under a bridge with a burning 55-gallon drum as the only source of heat. He is such a sadist. I was nearly frazzled with stress trying to raise the standard of our living.

I prayed, or more accurately, I complained to God. I explained to Him how I was living closer to Him than I had ever lived and yet we were suffering with utility bills and lack of groceries. I wondered, "Where are You, Lord!" I was a preacher and a pastor. All the other men of God seemed to have abundance, yet I was in need. My car looked so bad that when we had guests in the church, one of my deacons volunteered to hide it for me behind the building. I watched my wife boil water to give us hot baths. The gas was off and sometimes the lights. I was preaching, singing, and shouting, but inside the tremors of an earthquake of frustration began to swell.

I remember the car broke down. It didn't have too far to break down because it already was at death's door. The only way to fix that car was to commit the body to the ground and give the engine to the Lord. At the time, though, I needed to get uptown to ask the electric company not to cut off the only utility I had left. I caught the bus to town. I walked into the office prepared to beg, but not prepared to pay. I pleaded with the young lady; I promised her money. Nothing seemed to move her, and she cut it off anyway. I was crushed. I had been laid off my job, and my church was so poor it couldn't even pay attention. I was in trouble. I walked out of the utility office and burst into tears. I don't mean the quiet leaking of the tear ducts, either. I mean a deluge of sobbing, heaving, quaking, and wailing. I looked like an insane person walking down the street. I was at the end of my rope.

To this melodramatic outburst God said absolutely nothing. He waited until I had gained some slight level of composure and then spoke. I will never forget the sweet sound of His voice beneath the broken breathing of my fearful frustration. He said, in the rich tones of a clarinet-type voice, "I will not suffer thy foot to be moved!" That was all He said, but it was how He said it that caused worship to flush the pain out of my heart. It was as if He were saying, "Who do you think that I am? I will not suffer thy foot to be moved. Don't you understand that I love you?" I shall never forget as long as I live the holy hush and the peace of His promise that came into my spirit. Suddenly the light, the gas, and the money didn't matter. What mattered was I knew I was not alone. He sat down beside me and we rode home smiling in each other's face. It was the Lord and I.

> *As one whom his mother comforteth, so will I comfort you; and ye shall be comforted in Jerusalem* (Isaiah 66:13).

Chapter 3

DELAYED BUT NOT DENIED

We will always have seasons of struggles and testing. There are times when everything we attempt to do will seem to go wrong. Regardless of our prayers and consecration, adversity will come. We can't pray away God's seasons. The Lord has a purpose in not allowing us to be fruitful all the time. We need seasons of struggle. These periods destroy our pride in our own ability and reinforce our dependency on the sufficiency of our God. What a shock it is to find that the same person who was fruitful at one period experienced struggle at other times. When God sends the chilly winds of winter to blow on our circumstances, we must still trust Him. In spite of our dislike for the blinding winds and the icy grip of winter seasons, there is a purpose for these temporary inconveniences.

The apostle Paul calls such times "...light affliction, which is but for a moment..." (2 Cor. 4:17). I say, "This too shall pass!" Some things you are not meant to change, but to survive. So if you can't alter it, then outlive it! Be like a tree. In the frosty arms of winter the forest silently refurbishes its strength, preparing for its next season of fruitfulness. Its branches rocking in the winds, the sap and substance of the tree go underground. It is not good-bye, though; in the spring it will push its way up into the budding of a new experience. Temporary setbacks create opportunities for fresh commitment and renewal. If you were to record your accomplishments, you would notice that they were seasonal. There are seasons of sunshine as well as rain. Pleasure comes, then pain, and vice versa. Each stage has its own purpose.

One of the greatest struggles I have encountered is the temptation to make permanent decisions based on temporary circumstances. Someone once said, "Patience is a tree whose root is bitter, but its fruit is sweet." The reward of patience is reflected in gradually not having to amend your amendments. Temporary circumstances do not always require action. I have found that prayer brings us into patience. Patience results from trust. We cannot trust a God we don't talk with. Do not misunderstand me; God needs men and women who are decisive. However, every situation shouldn't get an immediate reaction. Prayer is the seasoning of good judgment. Without it, our decisions will not be palatable.

> *For the vision is yet for an appointed time, but at the end it shall speak, and not lie: though it tarry, wait for it; because it will surely come, it will not tarry* (Habakkuk 2:3).

Our struggle is in waiting for the appointment we have with destiny. Perhaps I should first point out that

God is a God of order; He does everything by appointment. He has set a predetermined appointment to bring to pass His promise in our lives. An appointment is a meeting already set up. Through the many tempestuous winds that blow against our lives, God has already prepared a way of escape. Our comfort is in knowing that we have an appointment with destiny. It is the inner awareness that makes us realize that in spite of temporary circumstances, God has a present time of deliverance.

We are enveloped in peace when we know that nothing the enemy does can abort the plan of God for our lives. Greater still is the peace that comes from knowing we cannot rush God's timing. When the Lord speaks a word into our lives, it is like a seed. It takes time for a seed to sprout. God knows when we have reached the time of germination. Our confidence is in God's seed. When the promise has grown in the fertile ground of a faith-filled heart and reached the time of maturation, it will come to pass. It will be a direct result of the presence of God. It will not be by human might or power, but by the Spirit of the Lord (see Zech. 4:6). The psalmist David said, "My times are in Thy hand" (Ps. 31:15a). For me there is a sense of tranquility that comes from resting in the Lord. His appointment for us is predetermined. There is a peace that comes from knowing God has included us in His plan—even the details.

I can remember as a very small child following close behind my mother, an educator in the public school system. She was often asked to speak at luncheons and banquets. Her sorority attracted the kind of successful ladies who had achieved academic and sociological accomplishments. These were the kind of ladies who extended their pinky fingers when they drank tea from china cups and saucers. These matronly madams of the 1960's prided themselves on being classy and distinguished. After the festivities had subsided and we were traveling from what I remember to be a rather stuffy atmosphere, I said to my mother, "Today, I travel with you and listen while you speak, but the time will come when you will travel with me and I will speak!" What was strange was this prophetic utterance came from the mouth of a then-devilish little six-year-old who, though very precocious, was nevertheless an ordinary child who would one day have a supernatural encounter with God!

I don't know how, at that early age, I knew I had an appointment with destiny, but I somehow sensed that God had a purpose for my life. I earnestly believe that everyone is predestined to accomplish certain things for the Lord. Somewhere in the recesses of your mind there should be an inner knowing that directs you toward an expected end. For me, it is this awareness that enables me to push myself up out of the bed and keep fighting for survival. You must be the kind of tenacious person who can speak to the enemy and tell him, "My life can't end without certain things coming to pass. It's not over until God says, 'It's over!'"

I don't think I really knew I would be a minister. I just felt that I would do something meaningful with my life. Twice in my childhood I spoke prophetically about things that have since come to pass. I can't say that everything I encountered in life pushed me toward my destiny. On the contrary, there were sharp contradictions as I went through my tempestuous teens. Still, I had that inner knowing, too deep to be explained. I want you to know that even if circumstances contradict purpose, purpose will always prevail! It is the opposition that clearly demonstrates to you that God is working. If the fulfillment of the prophecy was without obstruction, you would assume you had merely received serendipity. However, when all indicators say it is impossible and it still occurs, then you know God has done it again.

Perhaps someone's child is veering away from what you believe to be his predestined end. Let me share a quote with you. Dr. Martin Luther King is noted to have paraphrased William Cullen Bryant this way: "Truth smashed down to the ground will rise again undaunted!" It may seem impossible, but God knows how to make all things work together for good to them that love the Lord (see Rom. 8:28). It is so important for parents to instill a sense of destiny in their children. Once they realize that they have immeasurable potential, there is no stopping them. I am not saying that they won't deviate from the path—all of us have done that. But thank God they have been given a path to deviate from. Many children today don't know what the path even looks like. When it is all said and done, they will, like the prodigal son, come to themselves!

In Genesis, the Lord promised Eve a seed. He said, "And I will put enmity between thee and the woman, and between thy seed and her seed; it shall bruise thy head, and thou shalt bruise his heel" (Gen. 3:15). When Eve produced what she may have thought to be the promised seed, there were real problems. Her eldest son, Cain, was extremely jealous of her younger son, Abel. In the heat of rage, Cain killed his brother. In one swoop of jealousy, all of Eve's dreams lay bleeding on the ground. Now her eldest son was a criminal on the run, and her younger son snuffed out in the prime of life. Bleak despair pressed upon the heart of this mother. She was supposed to be the mother of all living and all she had raised was a corpse and its murderer.

But God unwrapped the blanket of failure from around her and blessed her with another son. His name she called "Seth." *Seth* means "substituted." It comes from the Hebrew root word *shiyth*, which means to appoint or place. Suddenly, as she held her new baby in her arms, she began to realize that God is sovereign. If He decrees a thing, it will surely come to pass. That doesn't stop the evil one from trying to delay the fulfillment of what God has said, but he can't stop it from happening. Your blessing may not come in the way you thought it would. It may not come through the person you thought it would. But if God said it, then rest assured. It may be delayed, but it cannot be denied. Eve called her third son "Seth," for she understood that if God makes a promise to bless someone, He will find a way! Even if it means appointing a substitute, He will perform His promise.

God's purpose was not aborted when Cain killed Abel. In spite of the fact that life has its broken places, ultimately everything God has ever said will come to pass.

Have you ever had to go through a time of attack? Satan tries to assassinate the will of God in your life. Nevertheless, He who has begun a good work in you shall perform it until the day of Jesus Christ (see Phil. 1:6). When we suffer loss like Eve did, there is a feeling of forlornness. However, you cannot allow past circumstances to abort future opportunity. If you have experienced loss in your life, I tell you that God has a way of restoring things you thought you would never see again.

> *And Adam knew his wife again; and she bare a son, and called his name Seth: For God, said she, hath appointed me another seed instead of Abel, whom Cain slew* (Genesis 4:25).

We come into this world fully cognizant of the fact that we have a limited amount of time. We don't live here for very long before we are confronted with the cold realities of death. From the loss of a goldfish to the death of a grandparent, all parents find themselves saddled with the responsibility of explaining why the pet or the person will not be coming back anymore. Yet what disturbs me most is not the quantity of life, but the quality of life. Simply stated, when death comes to push me through its window from time into eternity, I want to feel as though I accomplished something worthwhile. I want to feel that my life made some positive statement.

The saddest scenario I can imagine would be to face death's rattling call and wonder what would have happened if I had tried harder. It would be terrible to look back over your life and see that the many times you thought your request was denied was actually only delayed. Life will always present broken places, places of struggle and conflict. If you have a divine purpose and life has put you on hold, hang on! Stay on the line until life gets back to you. If you believe as I do, then it's worth the wait to receive your answer from the Lord.

> *I waited patiently for the Lord; and He inclined unto me, and heard my cry. He brought me up also out of an horrible pit, out of the miry clay, and set my feet upon a rock, and established my goings. And He hath put a new song in my mouth, even praise unto our God: many shall see it, and fear, and shall trust in the Lord* (Psalm 40:1-3).

The real test of faith is in facing the silence of being on hold. Those are the suspended times of indecision. Have you ever faced those times when your life seemed stagnant? Have you felt you were on the verge of something phenomenal, that you were waiting for that particular breakthrough that seemed to be taunting you by making you wait? All of us have faced days that seemed as though God had forgotten us. These are the moments that feel like eternity. These silent coaches take your patience into strenuous calisthenics. Patience gets a workout when God's answer is no answer. In other words, God's answer is not always yes or no; sometimes He says, "Not now!"

It is God's timing that we must learn. He synchronizes His answers to accomplish His purpose. Recently, while traveling on a major American airline, we were told that the plane could not land at its scheduled time. Evidently the air traffic controller instructed that we should wait in the air. What a strange place to have to wait—in the air! I have often felt like that aircraft suspended in the air when God says, "Wait!" Then the captain spoke into the PA system. He said, "We are going to assume a holding pattern until further instructions come from the tower." After some time, a few, rather intoxicated passengers began to question the traffic controller's decision. Perhaps we were all concerned. It's just that some had their concern lubricated with several stiff shots of rum!

The anxious looks and acidic remarks that came from the crowd subsided as the stewardess quickly eased people's fears. She informed several worried passengers that the planes always carry enough fuel to withstand the demands of these kinds of delays. There was a calm assurance on the faces of the attendants. I would have to attribute it to the fact that they had prepared for a delay. I began to wonder if we as the children of God shouldn't be better prepared for those times in our lives when God speaks from His throne, "Assume a holding pattern until further notice." The question is not always, "Do you have enough faith to receive?" Sometimes it is this: "Do you have enough faith to assume a holding pattern and wait for the fulfillment of the promise?"

You feel a deep sense of contentment when you know God has not forgotten you. I will never forget the time I went through a tremendous struggle. I thought it was an emergency. I thought I had to have an answer right then. I learned that God isn't easily spooked by what I call an emergency. While struggling in my heart to understand why He had not more readily answered my request, I stumbled upon a word that brought streams into my desert.

> *But God remembered Noah and all the wild animals and the livestock that were with him in the ark, and He sent a wind over the earth, and the waters receded* (Genesis 8:1 NIV).

The first four words were all I needed. I still quote them from time to time. When you realize that God knows where you are and that He will get back to you in time— what peace, what joy! Before Noah ran out of resources and provisions, God remembered him! The Lord knows where you are and He knows how much you have left in reserve. Just before you run out, God will send the wind to blow back the waters of impossibility and provide for you.

I can't begin to describe the real ammunition I received out of those four powerful words: *But God remembered Noah!* I too need ministry to keep my attitude from falling while I wait on the manifestation of the promise of God. Sometimes very simplistic reminders that God is still sovereign bring great joy to the heart of someone who is in a holding pattern. The comforting Spirit of God calms my fears every time He reminds me that God doesn't forget.

When working with people, we often must remind them that we are still there. They seem to readily forget who you are or what you did. God doesn't! Don't confuse your relationship with Him with your relationship with people. God says, through Paul, that it is unrighteous to forget. God simply doesn't forget. He has excellent records.

For God is not unrighteous to forget your work and labour of love, which ye have shown toward His name, in that ye have ministered to the saints, and do minister (Hebrews 6:10).

God's records are so complete that the hairs on your head are numbered (see Matt. 10:30). They are not just counted. Counted would mean He simply knows how many. No, they are numbered, meaning He knows which hair is in your comb! You know He has chronological records of your hair strands. Then you should know He has your family, your tithes, and your faithfulness in His view. How much more would God watch over you, if He already watches the numerical order of your hair? No wonder David declares, "What is man, that Thou art mindful of him?" (Ps. 8:4a) My friend, God's mind is full of you. Even in those moments of absolute stagnation in your life, He is working an expected end for your good (see Jer. 29:11).

When Noah had been held up long enough to accomplish what was necessary for his good, God sent the wind. There is a wind that comes from the Presence of God. It blows back the hindrances and dries the ground beneath your feet. The wind of the Holy Spirit often comes as a sign to you from the control tower. You have been cleared for a landing! Whenever the breath of the Almighty breathes a fresh anointing on you, it is a divine indication of a supernatural deliverance.

Regardless of the obstacle in your life, there is a wind from God that can bring you out. Let the wind of the Lord blow down every spirit of fear and heaviness that would cause you to give up on what God has promised you. The description of the Holy Spirit says He is as "a rushing mighty wind" (Acts 2:2). For every mighty problem in your life, there is a mighty rushing wind! Now, a normal wind can be blocked out. If you close the door and lock the windows, the wind just passes over without changing the building. But if the wind is a mighty rushing wind, it will blow down the door and break in the windows. There is a gusty wind from the Lord that is too strong to be controlled. It will blow back the Red Sea. It will roll back the Jordan River. It will blow dry the wet, marshy, flooded lands as in the days of Noah. God's wind is still ultraeffective against every current event in your life.

Chapter 4

REFINER'S FIRE

We often face discouragement in this world. Many have never had anyone who believed in them. Even after achieving some level of success in one area or another, many have not had anyone to point out their potential. Isn't it amazing how we can see so much potential in others, yet find it difficult to unlock our own hidden treasure? Highly motivated people are not exempt from needing someone to underline their strengths and weaknesses. It is impossible to perceive how much stronger we might be if we had had stronger nurturing. Nurturing is the investment necessary to stimulate the potential that we possess. Without nurturing, inner strengths may remain dormant. Therefore it is crucial to our development that there be some degree of nurturing the intrinsic resources we possess.

There is a difference in the emotional makeup of a child who has had a substantial deposit of affection and affirmation. Great affirmation occurs when someone invests into our personhood. I believe that people are the greatest investments in the world. A wonderful bond exists between the person who invests and the one in whom the investment is made. This bond evolves from the heart of anyone who recognizes the investment was made before the person accomplished the goal. Anyone will invest in a sure success, but aren't we grateful when someone supports us when we were somewhat of a risk?

Although it is true that fire will not destroy gold, it is important to note that fire purifies the gold. When God gets ready to polish His gold, He uses fiery trials. Unfortunately, nothing brings luster to your character and commitment to your heart like opposition does. The finished product is a result of the fiery process. Whenever you see someone shining with the kind of brilliancy that enables God to look down and see Himself, you are looking at someone who has been through the furnace of affliction.

Let me warn you: God places His prize possessions in the fire. The precious vessels that He draws the most brilliant glory from often are exposed to the melting pot of distress. The bad news is, even those who live godly lives will suffer persecution. The good news is, you might be in the fire, but God controls the thermostat! He knows how hot it needs to be to accomplish His purpose in your life. I don't know anyone I would rather trust with the thermostat than the God of all grace.

Every test has degrees. Some people have experienced similar distresses, but to varying degrees. God knows the temperature that will burn away the impurities from His purpose. It is sad to have to admit this, but many times we release the ungodliness from our lives only as we experience the dread chastisement of a faithful God who is committed to bringing about change. How often He has had to fan the flames around me to produce the effects that He wanted in my life. In short, God is serious about producing the change in our lives that will glorify Him.

> *I indeed baptize you with water unto repentance: but He that cometh after me is mightier than I, whose shoes I am not worthy to bear: He shall baptize you with the Holy Ghost, and with fire: whose fan is in His hand, and He will thoroughly purge His floor, and gather His wheat into the garner; but He will burn up the chaff with unquenchable fire* (Matthew 3:11-12).

His hand has fanned the flames that were needed to teach patience, prayer, and many other invaluable lessons. We need His corrections. We don't enjoy them, but we need them. Without the correction of the Lord, we continue in our own way. What a joy to know that He cares enough to straighten out the jagged places in our lives. It is His fatherly corrections that confirm us as legitimate sons and not illegitimate ones. He affirms my position in Him by correcting and chastening me.

> *But if ye be without chastisement, whereof all are partakers, then are ye bastards, and not sons* (Hebrews 12:8).

Strong's #G3541 "*nothos* (noth'os); of uncertain affinity; a spurious or illegitimate son:—bastard."

It is impossible to discuss the value of investing in people and not find ourselves worshiping God—what a perfect picture of investment. God is the major stockholder.

No matter who He later uses to enhance our characters, we need to remember the magnitude of God's investment in our lives. The greatest primary investment He made was the inflated, unthinkable price of redemption that He paid. No one else would have bought us at that price. He paid the ultimate price when He died for our sins. What He did on the cross was worship. According to *Nelson's Bible Dictionary*, the word *worship*, literally translated, means "to express the worth of an object." Normally the lesser worships the greater, but this time, the greater worshiped the lesser. What an investment!

Explore with me the concept that God has an investment in our lives. First of all, no one invests without the expectation of gain. What would a perfect God have to gain from investing in an imperfect man? The apostle Paul wrote, "But we have this treasure in earthen vessels, that the excellency of the power may be of God, and not of us" (2 Cor. 4:7) Thus, according to Scripture, we possess treasure. However, the excellency of what we have is not of us, but of God. The treasure is "of" God. That implies that this treasure originates from God. It is accumulated in us and then presented back to Him. No farmer plants a field in the ground because he wants more earth. No, his expectation is in the seed that he planted. The ground is just the environment for the planted seed. The seed is the farmer's investment. The harvest is his return, or more accurately, his inheritance as the outer encasement of the seed dies in the ground. Harvest cost the seed its life.

Verily, verily, I say unto you, Except a corn of wheat fall into the ground and die, it abideth alone: but if it die, it bringeth forth much fruit (John 12:24).

We are that fertile ground—broken by troubles, enriched by failures, and watered with tears. Yet undeniably there is a deposit within us. This deposit is valuable enough to place us on satan's hit list. In writing to the Ephesian church, Paul prayed that "the eyes of your understanding being enlightened..." (Eph. 1:18). One of the things he wanted the people to know is the riches of His inheritance in the saints! Paul challenged them to become progressively aware of the enormity of His inheritance in us, not our inheritance in Him. We spend most of our time talking about what we want from God. The real issue is what He wants from us. It is the Lord who has the greatest investment. We are the parched, dry ground from which Christ springs. Believe me, God is serious about His investment!

To the enemy the Lord says, "Touch not Mine anointed, and do My prophets no harm" (1 Chron. 16:22). God will fight to protect the investment He has placed in your life. What a comfort it is to know that the Lord has a vested interest in my deliverance. He has more than just concern for me. God has begun the necessary process of cultivating what He has invested in my life. Have you ever stopped to think that it was God's divine purpose that kept you afloat when others capsized beneath the load of life? Look at Job; he knew that God had an investment in his life that no season of distress could eradicate.

> *But He knoweth the way that I take: when He hath tried me, I shall come forth as gold* (Job 23:10).

Remember the story of the three Hebrew boys in the fiery furnace? When the wicked king placed them in the fire, he thought the fire would burn them. He didn't know that when you belong to God, the fire only burns the ties that bind you. People have said that God took the heat out of the furnace. That is not true. Consider the soldiers who threw the Hebrews into the fire—they were burned to death at the door! There was plenty of heat in the furnace. God, however, controls the boundaries. Have you ever gone through a dilemma that should have scorched every area of your life and yet you survived the pressure? Then you ought to know that He is Lord over the fire!

It has been suggested that if you walk in the Spirit, you won't have to contend with the fire. Real faith doesn't mean you won't go through the fire. Real faith simply means that when you pass through the fire, He will be with you. This thought brings you to an unusual reality. In most cases, if I told you that tomorrow you would be burned alive, but not to worry because I would be in the fire with you, my presence in the dilemma would provide no comfort at all. Yet the presence of the Lord can turn a burning inferno into a walk in the park! The Bible says a fourth person was in the fire, and so the three Hebrews were able to walk around unharmed in it (see Dan. 3).

King Nebuchadnezzar was astonished when he saw them overcome what had destroyed other men. I cannot guarantee that you will not face terrifying situations if you believe God. I can declare that if you face them with

Christ's presence, the effects of the circumstance will be drastically altered. It is quite popular to suggest that faith prohibits trouble. But when I read about these young Hebrew men, I realize that if you believe God, you can walk in what other men burn in. Seldom will anyone fully appreciate the fire you have walked through, but be assured that God knows the fiery path to accomplishment. He can heal the blistered feet of the traveler.

When John was on the isle of Patmos, he was limited to a cave but free in his spirit (see Rev. 1). Remember, satan may work feverishly to limit the ministry and reputation of God's vessel, but he can never confine the anointing and the call on your life. In fact, John's predicament on Patmos proves that negative circumstances reveal Christ, not veil Him. While in the dank, dismal, dark caves of persecution, surrounded by the sounds of other abused prisoners, John caught a vision. In his newfound image of Christ, he describes the crisp clarity of a revelation given in the midst of chaos. A crisis can clear your perceptions as you behold His face, looking for answers that will not be found in the confines of the situation.

Every ministry gift will eventually confront the cave of loneliness and the prison of an ostracized situation. Nevertheless, let the jailer beware; our God has a prison ministry. He explodes the walls of impossibility. John wrote that he heard the thunderous voice of the Lord. In the process of seeking the voice, he encountered seven golden candlesticks. The candlesticks are later revealed as the Church. We need men and women who hear the voice of God before they see the work of God. What good will it do us to polish the candelabra and light the candles if there is no voice of God to cause men to turn aside and see?

When the voice of God led to the presence of Christ, John collapsed in the presence of the Lord. A deluge flooded the cave as Christ opened His mouth; His voice sounded as the noise of many waters. John said that many waters were in His voice, but the fire was on His feet. Effective communication is always transmitted from the base of burned feet. John said Jesus' feet looked as if they had been in the fire. What a comfort to the indicted character of this Pentecost preacher to find that the feet of his Consoler had been through the fire. Dearly beloved, hear me today: Your Deliverer has feet that have been burned. He knows what it feels like to be in the fire.

Thank God for the smoldering feet of our Lord that run swiftly to meet His children in need. But still the question remains, "Is there any preventive protection that will at least aid the victim who struggles in the throes of a fiery test?" If you are in a fiery trial, be advised that it is your faith that is on trial. If you are to overcome the dilemma, it will not be by your feelings, but by your faith. First John 5:4 says, "For whatsoever is born of God overcometh the world: and this is the victory that overcometh the world, even our faith." Yes, it is the shield of faith that quenches the fiery darts of the devil (see Eph. 6:16). The term *quench* means "to extinguish." Are there any fires brewing that you would like to extinguish? Your faith will do the job. If faith doesn't deliver you from it, then it will surely deliver you through it.

The fanaticism of some faith theology has intimidated many Christians from faith concepts as they relate to the promises of God. Yet faith is such a key issue for the Christian that the people of the early Church were simply called believers in recognition of their great faith. One thing we need to do is understand the distinctions of faith. Faith cannot alter purpose; it only acts as an agent to assist in fulfilling the predetermined purpose of God. If God's plan requires that we suffer certain opposition in order to accomplish His purpose, then faith becomes the vehicle that enables us to persevere and delivers us through the test. On the other hand, the enemy afflicts the believer in an attempt to abort the purpose of God. Faith is a night watchman sent to guard the purpose of God. It will deliver us out of the hand of the enemy—the enemy being anything that hinders the purpose of God in our lives.

> *From that time on Jesus began to explain to His disciples that He must go to Jerusalem and suffer many things at the hands of the elders, chief priests and teachers of the law, and that He must be killed and on the third day be raised to life. Peter took Him aside and began to rebuke Him. "Never, Lord!" he said. "This shall never happen to You!" Jesus turned and said to Peter, "Get behind Me, Satan! You are a stumbling block to Me; you do not have in mind the things of God, but the things of men"* (Matthew 16:21-23 NIV).

Hebrews chapter 11 discusses at length the definition of faith. It then shares the deeds of faith in verses 32-35a and finally it discusses the perseverance of faith in verses 35b-39. There are distinctions of faith as well. In Hebrews

51

11:32-35a, the teaching has placed an intensified kind of emphasis on the distinct faith that escapes peril and overcomes obstacles.

> *Quenched the violence of fire, escaped the edge of the sword, out of weakness were made strong, waxed valiant in fight, turned to flight the armies of the aliens* (Hebrews 11:34).

However, in the verses that end the chapter, almost as if they were footnotes, the writer deals with the distinctions of another kind of faith. In his closing remarks, he shares that there were some other believers whose faith was exemplified *through* suffering and not *from* suffering.

> *And others had trial of cruel mockings and scourgings, yea, moreover of bonds and imprisonment: they were stoned, they were sawn asunder, were tempted, were slain with the sword: they wandered about in sheepskins and goatskins; being destitute, afflicted, tormented* (Hebrews 11:36-37).

Christianity's foundation is not built upon elite mansions, stocks and bonds, or sports cars and cruise-control living. All these things are wonderful if God chooses to bless you with them. However, to make finances the symbol of faith is ridiculous. The Church is built on the backs of men who withstood discomfort for a cause. These men were not the end but the means whereby God was glorified. Some of them exhibited their faith through their shadows' healing sick people. Still others exhibited their faith by bleeding to death beneath piles of stone. They also had a brand of faith that seemed to ease the effects, though it didn't alter the cause.

There are times in our lives when God will take us from one realm of faith to another. There are multiplicities of fiery trials, but thank God that for every trial there is a faith that enables us. Christ is the Author and the Finisher of our faith (see Heb. 12:2). He knows what kind of heat to place upon us to produce the faith needed in the situation. Remember, when we present our bodies as living sacrifices, He is the God who answers by fire. The good news lies in the fact that when our faith collapses beneath the weight of unbelievable circumstances, He gives us His faith to continue on.

> *I am crucified with Christ: nevertheless I live; yet not I, but Christ liveth in me: and the life which I now live in the flesh I live by the faith of the Son of God, who loved me, and gave Himself for me* (Galatians 2:20).

The space in this book is too limited to allow us the privilege of discussing the gift of faith and its function in the overall profile of the New Testament Church. But it is true that all faith is a gift from God!

As the fire of persecution forces us to make deeper levels of commitment, it is so important that our faith be renewed to match our level of commitment. There is a place in God where the fire consumes every other desire but to know the Lord in the power of His resurrection. At this level all other pursuits tarnish and seem worthless in comparison. Perhaps this is what Paul really pressed toward, that place of total surrender. Certainly that is the place I reach toward, which often escapes my grasp, but never my view. Like a child standing on his toes, I reach after a place too high to be touched. I conclude by saying my hands are extended, but my feet are on fire!

> *Yea doubtless, and I count all things but loss for the excellency of the knowledge of Christ Jesus my Lord: for whom I have suffered the loss of all things, and do count them but dung, that I may win Christ, and be found in Him, not having mine own righteousness, which is of the law, but that which is through the faith of Christ, the righteousness which is of God by faith: that I may know Him, and the power of His resurrection, and the fellowship of His sufferings, being made conformable unto His death* (Philippians 3:8-10).

Chapter 5

I Am Come in My Father's Name

Tinkling gently in the night, a child's mobile turns in the stillness. It is, to the gentle bundle of love beneath it, a million miles away. Wrapped in clean crisp sheets below the mobile is a mystery of creation. Stardust is sprinkled in the eyes of the child wandering in and out of sleep. Baby's soft gurgle blends with the occasional tinkling sounds of its overhead entertainment. Time has hidden the future of the baby deeply within the tiny hands that someday will be different things to different people. "Who is this child?" the parents ponder. "When we are old, who will this child be? What is the level of contribution we have given to this world?" All these questions are raised in the stillness of the night. Time listens quietly, patting its foot, but still offers no answer.

We toddle through childhood, from tricycles to training wheels, racing into the maze of adolescence. Too old to be a child, yet too childlike to be an adult, we often feel lost in space. The haunting question dulls with time, but still hums beneath the mind of the mature. "Who am I?" We have a deep need to find some answer for that question. A friend once told me that the best way to hold someone's attention in a conversation is to talk about that person! We are very interested in ourselves. Many of us come to know the Lord because we desperately need to know ourselves. Does that seem strange? It isn't, really. If we have a problem with an appliance, we always refer to the owner's manual. In our case it's the Bible. When repairs are needed, we go to the Manufacturer. Psalm 100 says, "It is He that hath made us, and not we ourselves" (Ps. 100:3b).

The Jacob in the Bible was one of God's great heroes. He was a limping leader graced to come to know who he was in a personal way. A struggler, Jacob wrestled with the only One who can give lasting answers to hard-hitting questions. He wrestled with God!

Jacob was his mother's darling. It was probably she who had given him his name. He was what we would call a "momma's boy." While Esau, his twin brother, hunted and killed game, Jacob baked cookies and tried new recipes. Softer, more timid, he might have been weak-wristed, but he was cunning and dangerous. It wasn't long before Jacob had learned how to be very manipulative and tricky. It was only when his trickery brought him to a dead end that he began to struggle with God for an answer.

Jacob, whose name meant "supplanter" or "trickster," literally "con man," was left alone with God. God cannot accomplish anything with us until we are left alone with Him. There, in the isolation of our internal strife, God begins the process of transforming disgrace into grace. It only took a midnight rendezvous and an encounter with a God he couldn't "out slick" to bring Jacob's leg to a limp and his fist to a hand clasped in prayer. "I won't let You go till You bless me," he cries. God then tells him what he really needs to know. He tells Jacob that he is not who he thinks he is. In fact, he is really Israel, a prince. (See Genesis 32:24-30.) My friend, when we, like Jacob, seek to know God, He will inevitably show us our real identity. The greatest riches Jacob would ever receive were given while he was alone with the Father. It was simply the Father's telling him his name!

Imagine how shocking it was for this almost dysfunctional person to find that he was not who he thought he was. Here everyone had been calling him something that he really wasn't. All of his life they had called him a trickster. They called him that morning, noon, and night. When they called him to dinner, they would say, "Hey, Jacob, come and eat," which meant, "Hey, trickster, come and eat." Jacob simply acted out what everyone had said he was. But with the grip of a desperate man he caught the horns of the altar of prayer and prayed until the Father gave him his real identity. He said to Jacob, "Your name is Israel, and as a prince you have wrestled with God" (see Gen. 32:28). You could be a prince and not really know it. My friend, if no one else knows who you are, God knows. If you pray, the Father will give you a name.

Becoming a Christian is not like becoming a Muslim, however. You don't have to change your name in order to be in the Church. I want you to understand that the new birth is not a change on your birth certificate; it is a change in your heart. When you are in the presence of God, He will remove the stench of your old character and give you a new one. In this sense we have a name change as it pertains to our character. This is not a work of man, or a typist on a birth certificate. This is a work of the *Holy Spirit*. In the Bible names were generally significant to the birth, as in *Isaac*, whose name meant "laughter." His mother broke into fits of laughter when she saw what God had done for her in the winter season of her life. On other occasions names were prophetic. The name *Jesus* is prophetic. It means "salvation." Jesus was born to save His people from their sins. In a few cases, the names were relative both to origin and prophecy. A keen example is that of *Moses*, whose name meant "drawn out." He was originally drawn out of the water by Pharaoh's daughter, but prophetically called of God to draw his people out of Egypt.

Understand then that a name is important. It tells something about your origin or your destiny. You don't want just anyone to name you. No one should want just anyone to prophesy over him without knowing whether or not that person is right. Words have power! Many of God's people are walking under the stigma of their old nature's name. That wretched feeling associated with what others called you or thought about you can limit you as you reach for greatness. However, it is not what others think that matters. You want to be sure, even if you are left alone and no one knows but you, to know who the Father says you are. Knowing your new name is for your own edification. When the enemy gets out his list and starts naming your past, tell him, "Haven't you heard? The person you knew died! I am not who he was and I am certainly not what he did!"

Mary, the mother of Jesus, had the baby, but the angel was sent from the Father to give the name. She couldn't name Him because she didn't fully understand His destiny. Don't allow people who don't understand your destiny to name you. They also probably whispered that Jesus was the illegitimate child of Joseph. Maybe there has been some nasty little rumor out on you too. Rumors smear the reputation and defame the character of many innocent people. However, none lived with any better moral character than Jesus—and they still assaulted His reputation. Just be sure the rumors are false or in the past and keep on living. I often say, "You can't help where you've been, but you can help where you're going."

In the chilly river of Jordan, with mud between His toes, it was the voice of the Father that declared the identity of Christ. His ministry could not begin until the Father laid hands upon Him by endorsing Him in the midst of the crowd. It is so important that we as sons receive the blessing of our spiritual fathers. I know countless preachers who ran away from their spiritual homes without their fathers' blessings and, even after many years, are still in a turmoil. If Jesus needed His Father's blessing, how much more do you and I? We should not seek to endorse ourselves.

Even though you have ten thousand guardians in Christ, you do not have many fathers, for in Christ Jesus I became your father through the gospel (1 Corinthians 4:15 NIV.)

We must know the difference between guardians and fathers. Paul said that he became their father through the gospel. For myself, I grew up in a church that had what we called "church mothers." These old saintly women prayed with fire and corrected us with the zeal of lightning. As awesome as they were, what were missing in the church were fathers. I don't necessarily mean men who carried the title of father, but men who spoke into the lives of other men with the unfeigned love of a father. We cannot take a nation of women and produce a nation of men. Everything basically reproduces after its own kind. Although that phrase in Genesis 1 refers to the creation, it has a larger application in terms of spiritual reproduction. Have you ever noticed that churches with a lot of men draw more men? Men do not always feel comfortable in a setting where there are no other men.

Many young men come into the church bleeding over their relationships—or lack of relationships—with their fathers. It is important that they be sired by pastors who can lay hands on them and affirm them by giving back to them their identity and self-esteem. Boys are nurtured by their mothers, but they receive their identity and definition of masculinity from their fathers! Thank God for the mothers in the Church—but where are our fathers? We have raised a generation of young men who couldn't find their natural fathers and now they struggle with their spiritual fathers. It is difficult to develop healthy spiritual authority in the heart of a man who hasn't seen healthy male relationships. Such men tend to be overly sensitive or rebellious, quickly associating authority with abuse as that may be their only past experience. To you men, whether younger or older, who still wrestle with these issues, allow the hand of your heavenly Father to heal the abuse and neglect of your earthly fathers. God is so wise that He will give you a spiritual father to fill the voids in your life. Trust Him!

So Jacob, now Israel, becomes a picture of an incapacitated leader who, through his struggles, has come to a point of resting in the presence of the Lord and his God-given identity. God's grace is so good at piloting those of us who walk through life on limping limbs. But now Israel has seasoned and matured. He has produced many strong sons. One son is yet in the loins of the love of his life, Rachel, who is in the final stages of pregnancy. Her husband is desperately trying to get her to Ephrath by wagon (see Gen. 35:16-18). Before they could reach their destination, Rachel goes into gut-wrenching contractions and out in the desert, she births a son. However, this scene is clouded by death who, hovering like a buzzard, stealthily creeps around the bed. Just before death claims another victim, Rachel looks at her baby and names him *Benoni*, which means "son of my sorrow." She closes her eyes in one final contraction, but this one is not for the baby. It is for the mother, and like a puff of smoke in the night, she is gone.

A weeping midwife holds the stained infant in her arms. He is all that remains of Rachel. Now Jacob limps up into the wagon. Finding his lovely wife gone and his son born, his emotions are scrambled like eggs in a pan. "What is, uh, what is his name?" he asks. The midwife's trembling voice responds, "She said he was Benoni, son of my sorrow." Jacob's eyes turn deeply within. Perhaps he remembers what a wrong name can do to a child. Whatever the reflection, he speaks with the wisdom that is born only out of personal experience. "He shall not be called Benoni, son of my sorrow. He shall be called *Benjamin*, son of my right hand. He is my strength, not my sorrow!" he declares. Guess whose name prevailed, Benjamin; you are who your father says you are.

> *And whatsoever ye do in word or deed, do all in the name of the Lord Jesus, giving thanks to God and the Father by Him* (Colossians 3:17).

In the name of Jesus you must break the spell of every name that would attach itself to you. If your heavenly Father didn't give you that name, then it isn't right. You are who He says you are. Rest in the identity that He places upon you. No one knew any better than Jacob/ Israel the power of a name change! Remember, it was in his Father's presence that he discovered he was not a trickster, but a prince! When you believe on the covenant name of Jesus, you break the strength of every other name that would attach itself to your identity. In the early Church, entire cities were delivered from satanic attack in that name. Even today, drug addicts, lesbians, pimps, and every other name is subject to the name of the Lord. His name is strong enough to break the bondage of any other name that would attach itself to your life.

> *Wherefore God also hath highly exalted Him, and given Him a name which is above every name: that at the name of Jesus every knee should bow, of things in*

heaven, and things in earth, and things under the earth (Philippians 2:9-10).

A good name is a very precious possession. It is often more lucrative than financial prosperity. If your name is associated with wealth, ministry, scandal, etc., then your name soon becomes synonymous with whatever it is most often associated. If I were to mention certain names, you would immediately think of Hollywood, wealth, or perhaps a certain university. Or I could refer to other names that would immediately conjure up images of mobs, murders, adultery, or deceit. The dilemma in which many people find themselves ensnared can be put like this: "How can I reverse the image or stigma that has been placed upon my name?" The names of some people are damaged because of past failures and indiscretions. Still others wrestle with the stains of rumors and the disgraceful, damaging, defamation of character. Whether or not a rumor is true does not matter; people prefer excitement and speculation.

Whether you have acquired an infamous name through being a victim or a villain, I have good news. If you are wrestling with the curse and stigma of public opinion, if people have categorized you for so long that you have accepted your origin for your prophecy—I still have good news for you. You don't have to stay the way you are. The Potter wants to put you back together again. Do you believe that God is a God of second chances? If you do, I want to unite my faith with yours, because I believe He gives second chances.

This good news is that God changes names. Throughout the Scriptures He took men like Abram, the exalted father, and transformed his image and character into *Abraham*, the father of many nations. *Jacob*, the supplanter, became *Israel*, the prince. A name is an expression of character; it means no more than the character behind it. Now, I don't want everyone to run to the courthouse and change his name. However, I do want you to realize that there is a place in your walk with God—a place of discipleship— whereby God radically changes your character. With that change He can erase the stigma of your past and give you, as it were, a fresh name in your community—but most importantly, in your heart. You see, my friend, when you were wandering in search of yourself like the prodigal son, God knew who you really were all the time. When you finally came to yourself, He was there. I recommend you get on your knees and wrestle with Him in prayer until you can arise knowing what He knows. Rise up from prayer knowing who you really are in the spirit and in the Kingdom.

Many of you are like Hananiah, Mishael, and Azariah. If you don't know them, perhaps you'll recognize them by the heathen names Nebuchadnezzar gave them: *Shadrach*, "command of Aku," *Meshach*, "pagan name," and *Abednego*, "servant of Nego." These names expressed worship to heathen gods, as defined by *Nelson's Bible Dictionary*. Their real names, however, were *Hananiah*, "Jehovah is gracious," *Mishael*, "who is like God," and *Azariah*, "Jehovah has helped." When the wicked king threw them into the fiery furnace, the names God called them prevailed!

There is nothing quite like trouble to bring out your true identity. Aren't you glad that you are not limited to public opinion? God's opinion will always prevail. Those three Hebrews came out of the furnace without a trace of smoke. That old king tried to change the name on the package, but he couldn't change the contents of the heart! Can you imagine those boys shouting when they came out? One would say, "Who is like God?" Another would lift his hands and say, "Jehovah is gracious!" The other would smell his clothes, touch his hair, and shout, "Jehovah has helped!"

If you have agonized on bended knees, praying at the altar to know the purpose and will of God for your life, and His answer doesn't line up with your circumstances, then call it what God calls it! The doctor might call it cancer, but if God calls it healed, then call it what God calls it. The word of the Lord often stands alone. It has no attorney and it needs no witness. It can stand on its own merit. Whatever He says, you are! If you are to fight the challenge of this age, then shake the enemy's names and insults off your shoulder. Look the enemy in the eye without guilt or timidity and declare:

> "I have not come clothed in the vesture of my
> past. Nor will I use the opinions of this world for
> my defense. No, I am far wiser through the things
> I have suffered. Therefore I have come in my
> Father's name. He has anointed my head, coun-
> seled my fears, and taught me who I am. I am
> covered by His anointing, comforted by His pres-
> ence, and kept by His auspicious grace. Today, as

never before, I stand in the identity He has given me and renounce every memory of who I was yesterday. I was called for such a time as this, and I have come in my Father's name!"

Chapter 6

ROMANCING A STONE?

So the man gave names to all the livestock, the birds of the air and all the beasts of the field. But for Adam no suitable helper was found (Genesis 2:20 NIV).

Attractions are allurements that can be based on memories, past experiences, and early associations. It is therefore very difficult to explain the extremely sensitive and fragile feelings that cause us to be attracted. Suffice it to say that we are instinctively attracted to inner needs. That attraction may be based upon a need to be with someone whom we think is attractive, which creates within us a certain validation of our own worth, or the attraction may be based on a deeper, less physical value. Either way, need is the fuel that spawns attraction. Opinions on what characteristics are attractive vary from person to person.

Most of us have had the unfortunate experience of being the victim of some matchmaking friend who inappropriately sets us up with someone who doesn't quite fit the bill. The blind date can be a terribly embarrassing situation. It is very difficult for even our close friends to predict who will attract us. I can remember contemplating the decision to marry. I sought the counsel of a very close friend. My friend told me, "I can't choose who will make you a good wife. Choosing a wife is one of the most personal decisions you will ever have to make—far too personal to accept the advice of people who will not have to live with the decision." Our friendship is still intact, and so is my marriage. Thank God for wise counsel.

Attractions, for many people, can be as deadly as a net to a fish. Seemingly, they can't see that the net is a trap until it is too late. They struggle, trying to get away, but the more they struggle, the more entangled they become. Like drug addicts, they make promises they can't keep, trying to pull away from something that holds them in its grasp like a vise. The key is not to struggle with the thing or the person. The deliverance comes from within and not from without. God is far too wise to put your deliverance into the hands of someone or something that may not have any compassion for you. The victory is won within the battleground of your mind, and its memories and needs.

Let's go even further. My children have a remote control toy car. The remote is designed so the car can be controlled even from a distance. The reason we can manipulate the car by an external item is the small apparatus inside the car that is affected by the remote control. If we remove the inner apparatus, the remote will not work. It is the same way with attractions. They evolve and manipulate us only because there is some inner apparatus that makes us vulnerable to them. If the wrong person, place, or thing controls our remote, we are in trouble. We may not be able to stop the person from playing with the buttons, but we can remove the inner apparatus.

We are communal by nature; we have a strong need for community and relationships. However, whatever we are in relationship with, we also are related to. It is important that we do not covenant with someone or something with which we are not really related. Every living being was created to pursue and cohabit with its own kind. I emphasize *kind*. There should be an agreement in species to achieve maximum compatibility. For instance, most men are incompatible with ducks. Right?

And God said, "Let the land produce living creatures according to their kinds: livestock, creatures that move along the ground, and wild animals, each according to its kind." And it was so. God made the wild animals according to their kinds, the livestock according to their kinds, and all the creatures that move along the ground according to their kinds. And God saw that it was good (Genesis 1:24-25 NIV).

Hence, we are forbidden from seeking intimacy, which is a legitimate need, from an inappropriate source. This is a biological law that governs biological order. If we break this law, we produce grossly disfigured, badly deranged, terribly mutated species that would give the normal mind nightmares. Whether or not a man is Christian, this law is still in effect. He can break it, but its penalties would be incomprehensible. What was introduced in the shadow of Old Testament theology as a biological law is magnified in the New Testament as a spiritual reality. In the Old Testament, each creature was mandated to bond with its own species. In the New Testament, the believer is commanded not to seek companionship outside the sanctity of the Church. Why? The Church is a species separate from any other, a species of which Christ is the firstborn.

> *Therefore, if anyone is in Christ, he is a new creation; the old has gone, the new has come!* (2 Corinthians 5:17 NIV)

We believers also are told in Second Corinthians 6:14 not to be unequally yoked with unbelievers. We are twice-born people; we are born and then born again. Now, it is not biologically illegal for us to bond with unbelievers; it is spiritually illegal. In the sight of God, yoking ourselves with unbelievers is spiritual *necrophilia*—having intimate relationships with the dead! To be a sinner is to be dead in sin!

> *And you hath He quickened, who were dead in trespasses and sins* (Ephesians 2:1).

As physical death is separation of the spirit and the body, so spiritual death, the state sinners are in, is the spirit of man separated from relationship with his Creator. Like Adam, he is hiding in the bushes of sin and covering himself with the fig leaves of excuses. This verse in Ephesians refers to the fact that sin is in itself a type of deadness of spirit. In the Scriptures, death doesn't mean the cessation of life. It clearly means separation. When a person dies physically, it is not the end of life; it is merely the separation of the body from the spirit. That's why James wrote, "Even so faith, if it hath not works, is dead, being alone" (Jas. 2:17). The Book of Revelation also refers to eternal damnation as the second death! (See Revelation 21:8.) It is called the second death not because existence or consciousness ends, but because it pronounces eternal separation from God. Without debating your concepts of hell, I am sure you would agree that eternity without God is a type of hell in itself. That is what the Book of Revelation calls the second death. It is eternal separation from the presence of God. It is the final step of sin. Sin is separation of relationship with God, but the second death is separation from the presence of God!

Let me make one final note about the spiritually dead, the sinners. They remind me of the bone-chilling horror movies we used to watch as children. Remember the sound of the wind sweeping through the trees? Then would come the shrill screeching of an old owl perched on a withered branch overlooking a poorly attended cemetery. Pushing through the soft, freshly turned soil, a hand emerged. By self-inflicted torturous tenacity, the corpse would exhume himself from the grave and stand up. I remember how in the sound track an old reedy organ would play a high note as on the screen appeared the bloody letters, "The Living Dead."

These zombies would walk the earth with their hands extended, always searching for but never attaining rest, leaving a trail of victims behind them. That's pretty ghoulish, but it is an accurate description of what sin is: "The Living Dead"! If you are an empty, brokenhearted person walking around always searching for things, for mere tokens of success, then I have a word from God for you. He says, "I am come that [you] might have life..." (John 10:10b). Accept Him today! Wake up from the nightmare of "The Living Dead" and become a living, loving testimony to the authenticity of the power of God!

When you are in sin, you reach after anything that will numb the pain and help you forget for a few minutes that something is missing. That doesn't work. It's God that's missing—a real relationship with Him. If you are missing Him, you can be reconciled to God at this very moment! The Bible makes the statement that you were dead in the trespass of sin (see Eph. 2:1). It teaches that you, as well as all of us, were separated from God because of sin. But God has reconciled His people to Himself. Being reunited with Him means I have life, and have it more abundantly (see John 10:10).

> *Remember that at that time you were separate from Christ, excluded from citizenship in Israel and foreigners to the covenants of the promise, without hope and without God in the world. But now in Christ Jesus you who once were far away have been brought near through the blood of Christ* (Ephesians 2:12-13 NIV).

This brings me to the fact that to be willfully disobedient and choose a companion who you know is dead in the trespasses of sin, is to be involved in spiritual necrophilia. Invariably, if you break a law, you reap a consequence. I am not referring to those who, while still a sinner, married another sinner, and then were converted. (At that point it is difficult for your partner to bridge the gap because he or she cannot fully *relate* to who you have become.) No, I am concerned for the precious hearts who find themselves attracted to others who haven't had this born-again experience. The person who willingly chooses to ignore God's stop signs is bound to experience adversity. The way of the transgressor is hard; it's not impossible, but quite difficult nonetheless. God's way is the best way. It's not His will for the living to marry the dead!

> *Be ye not unequally yoked together with unbelievers: for what fellowship hath righteousness with unrighteousness? and what communion hath light with darkness?* (2 Corinthians 6:14)

Now let's settle down to the deeper truths. The central concept is to avoid intimate contact with dead things. This message may get morbid, but let's take the concept further. Consider someone who has lost a loved one. This person has lost someone whom he or she had once been connected to and involved with. Now the beloved has expired. Grief-ridden and upset, the one left behind wishes with all of his or her might to be with that person again. The acidic taste of despair fills his or her mouth and wrenches his or her face into a pain-filled expression.

These rigid limbs will not move toward nor hold close anyone again. This cold, clay house that was once the dwelling place of affection and attraction has become as lifeless as a ceramic jar on a shelf. Once a person is dead, he is somehow strangely unfamiliar. At best he reflects a mere shadow of the once vibrant life. Empty eyes stare into the abyss of eternity, looking at what only death's victims can see. Even when the eyelids are closed, like drapes shut for the evening, there is a feeling that beneath the eyelids the eyes are still staring.

That fatal breath, expelled in a final gasp, blares an alarm that the former days are ended and the turning point has come. Who can change what has been done? It is finished. Like the end of a concerto, there is a note of finality that says to all in the room that the masterpiece is completed and the curtain is closed. Always soon afterwards there is an exodus as the living leave. No matter how much we weep and moan, eventually we file out of the room like the audience at the end of a concert. There is no further need to sit by the bed of the deceased. As long as there is life, we sit by the bed and hold the hands of the patient. When death has snatched them out of our grasp, though, it seems futile to sit where there is no sense of being together. Even though we are in the room with the corpse, we soon realize that we are very alone. The other person is not there; he is gone.

How unthinkable it would be, for instance, for a grief-stricken widow to stay behind to spend one final night in trying to move those icy arms into an embrace. It would be difficult to excuse her actions just because she was in love with someone who had died. The real disgust is in thinking that she could be attracted to something so morbid. How could she find arousal in the crisp touch of a cold clay doll? Regardless of what the relationship was at one time, surely she would recognize that death changes the reality—not the memory, but certainly the reality.

Who would walk past a casket in a funeral home and wink at a corpse? The very idea wavers between being disgusting and hilarious! What type of mind could not grasp the fact that this is inappropriate behavior for intelligent human beings? No widower would take his deceased wife out for a final weekend of romance. Romancing a stone? I should think not!

If this whole idea is so terrible, and it is, then why would born-again Christians who have been made alive by the power of God, go back into their own past and rummage through the graveyard of circumstances that God says are dead and over with? Why continue to embrace what ought to be buried? Regardless of how alive the event was at the time, when God says it is dead, then it is dead! How strange it must be in the spirit world for you, a living soul, to be wrapped up with a dead issue you have not yet relinquished.

There is a spirit of necrophilia eating at the hearts of many Christians. It is not so much the literal act of having intercourse with the dead. No, satan is far too subtle for that. Nor is it just a matter of people filled with the life of God purposely disobeying His Word and entering into covenant with the dead, sinful lives of unbelievers and calling it holy matrimony. Whether we admit it or not, we know that an unholy alliance cannot produce holy matrimony. No, the subtle serpent has gone deeper than that! He has many wonderful, well-meaning Christians praising, worshiping, and going to church, but in the stillness of the night, when no one is around, they lie in bed in the privacy of their homes, pull out guilt, scars, and memories, and play with the dead. If it's dead—and it is—then bury it!

> *Brethren, I count not myself to have apprehended: but this one thing I do, forgetting those things which are behind, and reaching forth unto those things which are before* (Philippians 3:13).

I once preached a message with a powerful title that I had heard years earlier. It was this: "Admit It! Quit It, and Forget It!" That's all you can do with the past, regardless of what it was or even who was at fault. When I say "forget it," that doesn't mean you actually lose awareness of the event. You don't have to be senile to be delivered! Rather, it means that you release the pain from the memory. The link that keeps you tied to what is past must be broken. In fact, I agree with you right now in the name of Jesus that those unsettled and unsettling issues that keep holding you in the night and affecting you in the light are broken by the power of God!

Intercourse brings two into oneness. Be careful what you allow to become one with you. You cannot continue to live in or be filled with the past. It is dead and over; break away from the intimate contact it would have on your life. Some things might never get resolved. They are like zombies walking around inside you all your life. Enough is enough! Everything that will not be healed must be forsaken. Really, to forsake it is to forget it. You cannot live in an intertwining embrace with something that God says you are to reckon as dead! Do not yield your body, your time, or your strength to this phantom lover! Tell that old corpse, "You can't touch this!"

> *Likewise reckon ye also yourselves to be dead indeed unto sin, but alive unto God through Jesus Christ our*

Lord. Let not sin therefore reign in your mortal body,
that ye should obey it in the lusts thereof. Neither yield
ye your members as instruments of unrighteousness
unto sin: but yield yourselves unto God, as those that
are alive from the dead, and your members as instru-
ments of righteousness unto God (Romans 6:11-13).

Thank God for the transparent testimony of the apostle Paul when he confided that all of his old issues were not yet laid to rest. Here he explains that there were moments when he was torn between who he wanted to become and who he used to be. Thank God for an honest testimony. Thank God for someone who tells the truth. We can hardly find a real witness anymore. We always tell how we came out, but we say nothing at all about how we went through! Paul, however, wasn't afraid of that pharisaical spirit that causes guilty men to be judgmental. He just said it plainly: "I am struggling with an old ghost that I want to be free from." Thank you, Paul, from all the rest of us would-be great men who thought there would be no struggle. Thanks for warning us—no, comforting us—with the honesty of your human aggravations.

O wretched man that I am! who shall deliver me from
the body of this death? (Romans 7:24)

Paul uses these terms to declare his struggles because he is wrestling with a corpse. One of the punishments decreed in Paul's day for certain types of criminals was capital punishment. But how they administered this death was quite bizarre. They would take the body of the murdered victim and tie it on the murderer. Thus everywhere the murderer went, the corpse did too, for it was attached to him. Worse still, the murdered victim was ever upon him—he could not forget his victim. He was weighted down by him. He could not avoid the putrid, rancid flesh to which he was attached. This kind of intimate contact would be unpleasant even if the man were alive, but because the man was dead, it was unbearable. The mere odor of the soft, decomposing, deteriorating flesh would reek with the stench of rot, contaminating all of life's moments with the ever-present aroma of decadence. What could we enjoy in life with this flesh hanging on as a sentinel from the past?

This nauseating level of intimacy with mushy flesh would turn the strongest stomach. That is exactly how Paul felt about the old nature that continued to press in so closely to his existence—rubbing him, touching him, always reminding him of things he could neither change nor eradicate. Eventually, for the punished murderer, this bacteria-filled, murky, mushy flesh would pass its fungus and disease to him until he died from this association with the dead. What an agonizing, disgusting way to die. When the apostle realized that his association with his past was affecting his present, he cried out, "O wretched man that I am! Who shall deliver me from so great a death?" That "who" rang throughout the heavenlies, searched the angels, and found no one worthy to answer the call. That "who" searched the underworld and found no one able to answer. It searched the earth—past, present, and future— and found a bleeding Lamb and an empty tomb. Then the angels cried, "Worthy is the Lamb! He is so worthy. Let Him untie you from this curse and be healed!"

You can live with those dead things hanging and clinging to you no better than Paul could. Allow the transforming power of God to rush through your life and cut the cord between you and your past. Whatever you do, remember to get rid of the old body. If the past is over, there is no need for you to walk around with mummies on your back—or should I say, on your mind! Get rid of that body and do it now! Those old memories will try to negotiate a deal, but you don't need a twin hanging on you. You don't need a secret affair with a corpse. You don't even need it as a roommate.

This is the time for an epitaph, not a revival. There are some things in life you will want to revive, but not this one. The past is something you want to die. It is always challenging for me as a pastor to assume the task of an eulogist at funerals. In order to effectively administer comfort and final services, you must know something of the relationship of the deceased to the family. It has been said that funerals are for the living, and I must totally agree with that thought. The funeral affords the remaining friends and loved ones an opportunity to resolve in their minds that the deceased is gone and that the relationship, as they had known it, is no more. Death doesn't seem to have the finality to a family that burial does. For some reason, until they officially put the deceased away, they seem to struggle with continuing their lives. Everything is placed on hold until the funeral is concluded.

I can still remember being a young man of 16 when they lowered my father into the cold Mississippi clay. I stood just over top of the grave looking down, face twisted in pain, confused and distraught. "This is it!" I thought. "He is absolutely gone!" I was devastated! But I also was aware that there is only one step between time and eternity, and that step was a lot shorter than I had thought. There is no hammer that presses the finality of death into the head of the onlooker like committing the body to the ground. Now the deceased loved one exists in brief shadows and glimpses, in memories that appear like dew on a pathway, wisps of moments envisioned, often as shadows. Philosophically, I know that my father exists in the very stroking of the computer as I write, and in the successes and failures of his children. Theologically, he exists somewhere in the great beyond where all Christians await the reunion that death has separated. But physically, there is no question about it; he is gone. Still, I have looked for him more often than I would ever confess!

There are some things you would like to have removed extremely far away. There are things I would like to lay to rest in such a definite way that they become merely fleeting wisps of fog faintly touching the recesses of the mind—gone, over, finished! It is those dearly departed, ghostly, painful issues of which I wrote. Suppose you took for a casket the truths discussed so far in this book, tossed all your concerns into the framework of God's Word, and committed to the ground everything that held you back from being healed and made whole. These phantom assassins are not to be trifled with; they must be laid to rest! This funeral, my friend, is not for them—it is you who must know it's over. Mark down this day as a record that it was this day you put away your nighttime playmates and moved into abundant life. Gather together all those villainous ghosts that desecrate the sanctity of what God would do in your life. Examine them. Cry if need be; scream if necessary—but when the service is over, bury every incident in the freshly turned soil of this word from God. Know that God has delivered you from playing with dead things.

> *Wherefore come out from among them, and be ye separate, saith the Lord, and touch not the unclean thing; and I will receive you* (2 Corinthians 6:17).

I am told that Mozart, one of the great composers of all time, sat late at night writing what was to be a masterpiece of symphonic excellence. Hours passed in the cozy quaint parlor where he worked, feverishly bent over the piano and then his notebook, writing and arranging with the compassion of a mother hovering over a dearly beloved child. Finally, as the sands of time poured silently through the glass and the heaviness of the day came crashing down upon his eyelids, he decided to stop and go to bed. Stumbling upstairs to his room, he changed with all the agility of a sluggish child who merely wants to go immediately to bed.

Strangely, once he was in bed, he found sleep evasive and he tossed and turned into the night. His work continued churning around in the chambers of his mind. You see, he had ended the symphony with an augmented chord. An augmented chord gives the feeling of waiting on something else to be heard. It is a feeling of being suspended over a cliff. Finally, when this composer could stand it no longer, he rose, tossed his wool plaid robe across his willowy shoulders, and stumbled down the steps. He went through all that to write one note. Yet how important that note was. It gave a sense of ending to the piece, and so was worth getting out of bed to write. People can never rest while living in a suspended mode. This composer then placed the quill back on his desk, blew out the lantern once more, and triumphantly retraced his way up the stairs and back to bed.

Now this great patriarch of symphonic excellence slipped into the bed with a feeling of satisfaction. He fluffed beneath his head the pillow that had once felt like a rock and just before the whistling wind outside his window ushered him into the sleep that only the peaceful can enjoy, he sighed faintly. Then his body gave way to the gentle caress of fatigue and he entered through the portal of tranquillity with the slightest hint of a smile hanging around the corners of his mouth. For him, the struggle was over.

In light of all that you have survived, it is high time that this same peace envelop you in a warm embrace and that the grace of understanding brush your lips with the kiss of peace in the night. You need to be like Jesus who dropped His head in the locks on His shoulders and said, "It is finished!" (See John 19:30.) It is time for that kind of benediction to be said in your life. Allow the God of all grace to give you the final rights that forever exorcise the dead from their secret place of intimate contact with you.

As this chapter closes, there is but one thing I would like to advise. You have the power. If you're finished with where you were, and you're ready for where you're about to go, then kiss your old ghosts good night. No, better still, kiss them good-bye. Their grasp is broken and you will see them no more.

> *Pharaoh's chariots and his host hath He cast into the sea: his chosen captains also are drowned in the Red sea. The depths have covered them: they sank into the bottom as a stone* (Exodus 15:4-5).

Chapter 7

OFFSPRING, ODDITIES, AND OBSTACLES

I will never forget in the early years of my pastoring, a particular church—or more accurately, a dream—that I pastored. This handful of members initially was the right number for inviting the whole church to almost anyone's house for dinner. That is an observation, not a complaint, because that handful was about all I could handle and, at the tender era of my early twenties, more than I could lead. I learned how to pray in those days of struggle and I gained a humility that prepared me for the things God would later do in my life. I remember certain situations that arose during that time which were all I could handle. I was very dependent upon God then, and I have never outgrown that deep need for His guidance.

Once a young lady, who had been attending my church, came to me in tears. She had been brutally raped by several young men. She was just a teenager. I was wounded to hear of this adversity that had left her feeling filthy, vile, and used. I was full of compassion, but not wisdom. I really didn't know what to say to her; I could only share her pain and pray for her future. She told me that the hospital gave her what they call a morning-after pill to stop the possibility of her being pregnant as a result of this tragedy. I later learned that this pill is designed to kill any possibility of pregnancy after rape. I scarcely knew how to counsel her, I was so afraid of saying the wrong thing. I realized that she could not undo what had been done. None of us could.

I mentioned her because I wish there was a spiritual morning-after pill we could get to kill the unwanted spiritual embryos left behind from our previous associations with dead things. Since we have succeeded in destroying our relationships with the past, let's deal with all those side effects that resulted from our previous infidelities. There can be progeny born in us from our relationships with the past; they must be sought out and destroyed. These offsprings of another time when we were less spiritually mature cannot be allowed to exist in us.

For instance, jealousy is the child of low self-esteem. Then there is always little tiny suicide wrapped in a blanket hiding in the shadows, born in the heart of a person who has been lying in bed with despair or guilt. Then there are people who habitually lie because fantasy seems more exciting than reality. Promiscuity, the child of a twisted need, has an insatiable appetite like that of greed's, which devours all whom it can touch. For all this, you weep through the night. But David said that if we could hold out, joy comes in the morning (see Ps. 30:5). The bad news is, everybody has had a bad night at one time or another. The good news is there will be a morning after. Allow the joy of the morning light to push away any unwanted partners, curses, or fears that stop you from achieving your goal.

So let the hungry mouth of failure's offspring meet the dry breast of a Christian who has determined to overcome the past. In order for these embryos of destruction to survive, they must be fed. They feed on the fears and insecurities of people who haven't declared their liberty. Like a horseleech, they are always sucking the life, the excitement, and the exuberance out of precious moments. The parent is dead; you have laid him to rest, but if not destroyed, the residue of early traumas will attach itself to your successes and abort your missions and goals. It nurses itself in your thought life, feeding off your inner struggles and inhibitions.

Once you realize that you are the source from which it draws its milk, you regain control. Put that baby on a fast! Feed what you want to live and starve what you want to die! Anything you refuse to feed will eventually die. You could literally starve and dehydrate those crying, screaming childhood fears into silence, security, and successful encounters. It's your milk—it's your mind! Why not think positively until every negative thing that is a result of dead issues turns blue and releases its grip on your home and your destiny? It's your mind. You've got the power!

Be careful for nothing; but in every thing by prayer and supplication with thanksgiving let your requests be made known unto God. And the peace of God, which passeth all understanding, shall keep your hearts and minds through Christ Jesus. Finally, brethren, whatsoever things are true, whatsoever things are honest, whatsoever things are just, whatsoever things are pure, whatsoever things are lovely, whatsoever things are of good report; if there be any virtue, and if there be any praise, think on these things (Philippians 4:6-8).

In this final summation of Pauline wisdom is some wonderful food for thought. In verse 6 he admonished the Philippians that prayer would produce the offspring of verse 7, which is peace. This is not just any peace, however; it is the peace of God that stands guard over the spirits and hearts of man like a night watchman keeping us from hysteria in a crisis. The apostle Paul swelled to a theological crescendo in verse 8 as he began to teach thought modification. He taught that if we exercise the discipline of thought modification, we can produce internal or intrinsic excellence. The phrase, "if there be any virtue," suggests that if there is to be any intrinsic excellence, we must modify our thoughts to think on the things he mentioned first.

Strong's #G703 "*arete* (ar-et'-ay); from the same as 730; properly, manliness (valor), i.e. excellence (intrinsic or attributed):—praise, virtue."

Don't be mystified by the term *virtue*. It refers to intrinsic excellence. That means people who are filled with excellence achieve that excellence by the thoughts they have about themselves and about the world around them. Thoughts are powerful. They feed the seeds of greatness that are in the womb of our minds. They also can nurse the negative insecurities that limit us and exempt us from greatness. There is a virtue that comes from tranquil, peaceful thoughts that build positive character in the heart. As a rule, people who are cynical and vicious tend to be unsuccessful. If they are successful, they don't really feel their success because their cynicism robs from them the sweet taste of reward.

Thoughts are secrets hidden behind quick smiles and professional veneers. They are a private world that others cannot invade. None of us would be comfortable at having all our thoughts played aloud for the whole world to hear. Yet our thoughts can accurately forecast approaching success or failure. No one can hear God think, but we can feel the effects of His thoughts toward us. Like sprouts emerging from enriched soil, our words and eventually our actions push through the fertilized fields of our innermost thoughts. Like our Creator we deeply affect others by our thoughts toward them.

> *For I know the thoughts that I think toward you, saith the Lord, thoughts of peace, and not of evil, to give you an expected end* (Jeremiah 29:11).

> *How precious also are Thy thoughts unto me, O God! how great is the sum of them!* (Psalm 139:17).

Stinking thinking is like the stench that came from the tomb of Lazarus. It is a result of interaction with dead things. Once the body is removed, however, the odor will eventually dissipate. There is a great need to clear the air in our minds because when the odor is left to cling, it can make the mind just as unpleasant as if the dead object was still there. I believe that's what makes preaching so powerful—it comes down and arrests the lingering odors and offspring of past experiences and removes them like old cobwebs from the sanctuary of our inner beings.

Some years ago I was birthing my ministry in terms of evangelism. I was peaching in places most up-and-coming ministers would not want to go. It was not at all uncommon for me to drive for hours into some rural, secluded "backwoods" area to minister to a handful of people who were often financially, and in some cases mentally, deprived! God teaches men character in the most deplorable of classrooms. So He had me in school. I thought I was traveling to minister to the people, but in actuality God was taking me through a series of hurdles and obstacles in order to strengthen my legs for the sprints ahead.

It was while on one of these pilgrimages into the unknown that I ministered in an area and then returned to the little place I was staying. The room I was given had a bed so bowed it looked like a musical instrument. The entire house was infested with flies. I have never before or after seen so many flies attracted to a house. I have often mused over the great possibility of satanic activity and witchcraft in that house. I can remember being horrified at the filth and slime that existed in the bathroom, and lying in my bed at night praying for the grace not to run.

While attempting to act as though I were comfortable in this inhumane environment, I encountered some children who came over to talk to me. I noticed immediately that most of them were either physically or mentally abnormal. These abnormalities ranged in severity from slurred speech to missing fingers and dwarfed limbs. Nevertheless, they were playing and laughing as children do who have been given the mercy of blindness to the wretchedness of their circumstances. One little boy came over and whispered in my ear. He said, "That little boy turning somersaults is my cousin-brother." It seemed that the little boy was the product of some hot summer night when need had overruled common sense and the little boy's mother had slept with her own brother and produced a mutated offspring that halted around as a testimony to their impropriety.

Suddenly I began to understand that these children were the result of inordinate affections and incestuous relationships! These are the twisted hands and stumped feet of children forever incapacitated by the sins of their parents. This plight is unnecessary; it could have been avoided. So are the children of the mind: the crippled need we sometimes have to receive the accolades of men; the twisted, angry tears that flood cold pillows in the night because we are left holding the offspring of yesterday's mistakes in our arms. Like a young girl left saddled with a child she can hardly rear, we wonder what we could have been if one thing or another had not happened.

There is a difference, however, between these natural children and the crippled ones that haunt the recesses of our minds. There is a difference between psychological and biological offspring. To abort a biological child is wrong. To abort psychological offspring is deliverance. I am not talking about aborting biological babies—I am talking about aborting every psychological baby that is growing in the womb of our minds. Every remaining embryo that ties us to a dead issue can be and must be aborted!

You don't have to leave some grossly deformed generation of problems that beget more problems! God has given you power over the enemy! This power is not rejoicing power, to sing or preach. It's not power over people and external dilemmas. He has given you the power to abort the seeds of failure. Abortion is a strong term, but effective in this case. Pull down the strongholds. Pull down those things that have taken a strong hold in your life. If you don't pull them down, they will refuse to relinquish their grip. It will take an act of your will and God's power to stop the spiritual unborn from manifesting in your life. God will not do it without you—but He will do it through you.

> *(For the weapons of our warfare are not carnal, but mighty through God to the pulling down of strong holds;) casting down imaginations, and every high thing that exalteth itself against the knowledge of God, and bringing into captivity every thought to the obedience of Christ* (2 Corinthians 10:4-5).

These thoughts, wounds, and emotional oddities are self-exalting. They establish themselves as god in your life. They endeavor to control or manipulate you. These progeny of lesser days want to crown themselves as indications of your destiny. How can you afford to submit your future to the discretion of your past? The greatest freedom you have is the freedom to change your mind. Enthroned in the recesses of your mind may be some antichrist that would desire to keep you connected to what you have forsaken. Cast it down! The Bible says to repent. Repentance is when the mind decides to organize a mutiny and overthrow the government that controlled it in the past. As long as these other things reign in your life, Christ's seat is taken because these thoughts and feelings of the past are sitting on the throne. If they are on the throne, then Christ is on the cross. Put Christ on the throne and your past on the cross.

In the special moments when thankful hearts and hands lifted in praise come into corporate levels of expression with memories of what could have happened had God not intervened, we find our real ministry. Above all titles and professions, every Christian is called to be a worshiper. We are a royal priesthood that might have become extinct had the mercy of the Lord not arrested the villainous horrors of the enemy. Calloused hands are raised in praise—hands that tell a story of struggle, whether spiritual or natural. These holy hands that we raise unto the Lord are the hands of people who, like Jonah, have lived through a personal hell. Who could better thank the Lord than the oppressed who were delivered by the might of a loving God whose love is tempered with the necessary ability to provoke change.

By Him therefore let us offer the sacrifice of praise to God continually, that is, the fruit of our lips giving thanks to His name (Hebrews 13:15).

If we are a priesthood, and we are, then we need an offering. There are many New Testament offerings that we can offer unto the Lord. As an induction into the office of the priest, we offered up our dead issues to a living Christ who quickened the pain and turned it into power! The intensity of our praise is born out of the ever-freshness of our memories, not so much of our past, but of His mercies toward us. The issue then is not whether we remember, but how we choose to remember what we've been through. He is able to take the sting out of the memory and still leave the sweet taste of victory intact. When that happens, we are enriched by our struggles, not limited.

Woe be to the priest who tries to have a fresh worship experience while constantly reliving the dead issues of the past. In that case the memories become an obstacle around your neck. Lift up your head and be blessed in the presence of the Lord. Nothing is nearly as important as ministering to the Lord. What would it matter for all the voices in the earth to harmoniously explode into accolades of appreciation commending you for your contributions, if God disagreed?

If we would reach new levels in worship, then we wouldn't be able to touch dead things! Instead they become obstacles that hinder us from deeper experiences in the Lord. In the early Church, the disciples experienced awesome displays of power that we don't seem to experience to the same degree. Few of us are walking in enough light to cast the kind of shadow that causes others to be healed. Our itinerary may take us from church to church, but the disciples traveled in the spirit from age to age and saw things that were not lawful to be uttered! What is wrong? We have become a nation of priests who spend too much time touching the dead and not enough washing our hearts with pure water!

> *He that toucheth the dead body of any man shall be unclean seven days. He shall purify himself with it on the third day, and on the seventh day he shall be clean: but if he purify not himself the third day, then the seventh day he shall not be clean. Whosoever toucheth the dead body of any man that is dead, and purifieth not himself, defileth the tabernacle of the Lord; and that soul shall be cut off from Israel: because the water of separation was not sprinkled upon him, he shall be unclean; his uncleanness is yet upon him* (Numbers 19:11-13).

Give your heart a bath. Submerge it deeply into the purity of God's Word and scrub away the remaining debris of deathly ills and concerns. These may be stopping you from participating in the greatest move of God that this generation will ever see! A clouded heart cannot move into the realm of faith. It takes clarity to flow in divine authority. Satan knows that pureness of heart is necessary to see God, to see the will of God, and to see the Word of God. You see, God's will is revealed in His Word. As for the Word, "...the Word was with God, and the Word was God" (John 1:1). These distresses and stresses are spiritual cholesterol! They will stop the heart from being able to see God.

If the priest, the worshiper, has so many unresolved issues on his heart, how can he see God? If he cannot see his God, his worship becomes routine and superficial. I can't help but wonder how much more we all would see of God if we would remove life's little buildups that clog the arteries of our hearts and not allow us to see the glory of God. These are the obstacles that keep us seeking the wisdom of men rather than the wisdom of God! These are the obstacles that make us feel insecure while we wait for an answer. These are the obstacles that keep many well-meaning Christians needing prayer rather than giving prayer. In short, let's clean out our hearts and we will hear, worship, and experience God in a new dimension. Clean out every thought that hinders the peace and power of God.

> *Blessed are the pure in heart: for they shall see God* (Matthew 5:8).

This Scripture clearly draws a line of prerequisites necessary to see God in His fullest sense. He is often described as the invisible God (see Col. 1:15). God's invisibility doesn't refer to an inability to be seen as much as it does to your inability to behold Him. To the blind all things are invisible. How can I see this God who cannot be detected in my vision's periphery? Jesus taught that a pure heart could see God. No wonder David cried out, "Create in me a clean heart..." (Ps. 51:10). The term used in Matthew 5:8 for *pure* comes from the Greek word *katharos*, which means "to clean out," much like a laxative. That may be funny, but it's true. Jesus is saying to give your heart a laxative when you've heard too much or seen too much. Don't carry around what God wants discarded. Give your heart a laxative and get rid of "every weight, and the sin which doth so easily beset us" (Heb. 12:1)! What God wants to unveil to you is worth the cleaning up to see.

From time to time when I minister I have a strange awareness of speaking directly to someone. I feel it now. Whoever you are, get ready for a fresh vision and a new move of God. Shake loose from everything that has kept your heart from seeing God. He is showing Himself. He is not hiding! Clean your heart out and clear your mind; He is there *now*!

I often build a fire on those cold wintry nights in West Virginia. Gathering the wood is a small price to pay once the logs have been ignited and that warm, engulfing glow of hot fire begins to reach out from the stove and fill the room with the soothing sound of crackling wood and the slight aroma of fresh fire. On those nights, when the day has taken its toll, I stare into the fire and watch it dance gleefully across the wood like children skipping on a hillside. Bursting up into the air, these occasional eruptions of sparks are nature's answer to fireworks, each group of sparks exploding into neon rainbows of splendor. It is a feast to weary eyes that need to be distracted into a lull of tranquillity.

While gazing deep into the fire you will notice that the sparks leave the burning log as hot as the fire itself. They swirl into the chimney with an angry ascension into the dark chambers above. But these flickering lights are soon extinguished by no other force than the aftereffects of being separated from their source. I thought, still staring silently into the glowing embers of the next fiery production,

"How many Christians explode into the brilliancy of worship and praise, but are soon dark and cold, losing their first fire." Stay in the fire, my friend, where the other embers can share their heat with you and keep you ablaze! It is the fire of God that will assist you in burning up the offspring, the oddities, and the obstacles of yesteryear.

Perhaps that is what happened in the fiery furnace with the Hebrew boys. Yes, there was a fire; I'm not denying that. But the fire was on assignment. It could burn only what was an obstacle hindering those who refused to worship idols from worshiping God. I don't know what they said as they walked around in the flames, observed by the king but preserved by the Lord! Perhaps they were saying what I feel compelled to share with you. Simply stated, some people He saves from the fire; praise God for them. But all too often God saves most of us by the fire!

> *If any man's work shall be burned, he shall suffer loss: but he himself shall be saved; yet so as by fire* (1 Corinthians 3:15).

Chapter 8

LIVING ON THE LEFT SIDE OF GOD

Behold, I go forward, but He is not there; and back-ward, but I cannot perceive Him: on the left hand, where He doth work, but I cannot behold Him; He hideth Himself on the right hand, that I cannot see Him (Job 23:8-9).

There are times when it is difficult to understand God's methods. There are moments when discerning His will is a frustrating endeavor. Perhaps we have these moments because we haven't been given all the information we need to ascertain His ways as well as His acts. Many times we learn more in retrospect than we do while in the thick of the struggle. I can look over my shoulder at my past and see that the hand of the Lord has been on me all my life. Yet there were times when I felt completely alone and afraid. Even Jesus once cried out, "Eli, Eli, lama sabachthani? that is to say, My God, My God, why hast Thou forsaken Me?" (Matt. 27:46b) Suspended on the cross with a bloody, beaten body, He was questioning the acts of God—but He never questioned His relationship with Him. Jesus says in essence, "I don't understand why, but You are still *My God!*"

I'm sure we have all felt our faith weighed down by a severe struggle that left us wondering what in the world God was doing. I can hardly believe that anyone who seriously walks with God has never felt like a child whose tiny toddling legs couldn't keep up with the strong stride of his parent. Sometimes I've thought, "Daddy, don't walk so fast." We can't see as well or move as quickly. It takes time to develop spiritual dexterity. To remain calm in crises and faithful in frightening times is easier said than done. Generally we see the workings of God when we look back, but while in the throes of the rumbling winds of life, we are often in search of the Lord.

Perhaps we are at our best when we are searching for Him; we have no independence, just raw need. There's no dawdling around with things that have no help or healing. Those are the times we know are jobs for God. If He doesn't help us, we will die.

The search for God is an "equal opportunity" experience for all Christians. Regardless of how successful you may be, you will always have times when you just need to find Him. Consecration is the Siamese twin of sanctification. They are born together and are connected. You can't be consecrated to without being sanctified from. Sanctification sets you apart from distractions, and consecration takes that separated person and quenches his thirst in the presence of the Lord!

As the hart panteth after the water brooks, so panteth my soul after Thee, O God. My soul thirsteth for God, for the living God: when shall I come and appear before God? My tears have been my meat day and night, while they continually say unto me, Where is thy God? When I remember these things, I pour out my soul in me: for I had gone with the multitude, I went with them to the house of God, with the voice of joy and praise, with a multitude that kept holyday (Psalm 42:1-4).

The search for God is a primary step into worship. We never search for anything we don't value. The very fact that we search for Him indicates that He has become essential to us. There are millions of people who seem to live their lives without noticing that something is missing. They seemingly sense no real void. Our separating ourselves from these ranks and saying, "God, I need You," is a form of worship. The word *worship* stems from the term *worth-ship*. It expresses the worth of an object. The kind of intensity that causes an individual to pursue the invisible in spite of all the visible distractions is a result of need. If we didn't need Him desperately, we could easily be satisfied with carnal things.

God instructs us to seek Him, but not as though He were hiding from us. He is not a child playing hide-and-go-seek. He isn't crouched behind trees giggling while we suffer. The request to seek Him is as much for our benefit as His. When we seek Him, we make a conscious decision that is necessary for bringing us into the realm of the spiritual. The pursuit of God is rewarding in the development of the seeker's character. Some levels of blessings are never received unless they are diligently sought. It is this seeking after God that often propels Him to perform. If that were not true, the woman with the issue of blood would never have been healed. Her conscious decision to seek the impossible released the invisible virtue of God.

> *But without faith it is impossible to please Him: for he that cometh to God must believe that He is, and that He is a rewarder of them that diligently seek Him* (Hebrews 11:6).

There are no manuals that instruct us step by step as to the proper way to seek the Lord. Like lovemaking, the pursuit is spontaneous and individually conceived out of the power of the moment. Some seek Him quietly, with soft tears falling quietly down a weary face. Others seek Him while walking the sandy beaches of a cove, gazing into the swelling currents of an evening tide. Some would raise their hands and praise and adore Him with loving expressions of adoration. There are no rules—just that we seek Him with our whole hearts.

We are like blind people when it comes to spiritual issues; we are limited. However, we should be challenged by our limitations. When there is a strong desire, we overcome our inabilities and press our way into His presence.

My friend, don't be afraid to stretch out your hands to reach after Him. Cry after Him. Whatever you do, do not allow this moment to pass you by!

> *And hath made of one blood all nations of men for to dwell on all the face of the earth, and hath determined*

the times before appointed, and the bounds of their habitation; that they should seek the Lord, if haply they might feel after Him, and find Him, though He be not far from every one of us (Acts 17:26-27).

Like groping fingers extended in the night trying to compensate for a darkened vision, we feel after God. We feel after His will and His ways. I'm amazed at all the people who seem to always know everything God is saying about everything. In the hymn "My Faith Looks Up to Thee," Ray Palmer and Lowell Mason wrote, "My faith looks up to thee, Oh lamb of calvary, savior divine." My faith looks up because my eyes can't always see. On the other hand, there is a healthy reaction that occurs in blindness; our senses become keener as we exercise areas that we wouldn't normally need.

God knows what it will take to bring us to a place of searching. He knows how to stir us from our tranquil and comfortable perching position of supremacy. There are times when even our great sages of this age murmur in the night. When the congregants have gone home and the crowd dissipates, there are moments in which even our most profound, articulate leaders grope in the dark for the plan and purpose of God. In spite of our strong gait and stiff backs, in spite of our rigid posture and swelling speech, behind the scenes we tremble in our hearts at the presence of God whose sovereign will often escapes the realm of our human reasoning.

Searching releases answers. The Word declares, "Seek, and ye shall find" (Matt. 7:7b). Many things available to us will not be found without an all-out search. Seeking God also takes focus. This search has to be what the police call an A.P.B. What does that mean? An *A.P.B.* is an "all points bulletin." All of the department is asked to seek the same thing. Thus our search can't be a distracted, half-hearted curiosity. There must be something to produce a unified effort to seek God. Body, soul, and spirit—all points— seeking the same thing. There is a blessing waiting for us. It will require an A.P.B. to bring it into existence, but it will be worth attaining. Who knows what God will release if we go on an all-out God-hunt.

I believe there are times when we grow weary of human answers. The crucial times that arise in our lives require more than good advice. We need a word from God. There are moments when we need total seclusion. We come home from work, take the telephone receiver off the hook, close the blinds, and lie before God for a closer connection. In Job's case, he was going through an absolute crisis. His finances were obliterated. His cattle, donkeys, and oxen were destroyed. His crops were gone. In those days it would be comparable to the crash of the stock market. It was as if Job, the richest man, had gone bankrupt. What a shock to his system to realize that all are vulnerable. It is sobering to realize that one incident, or a sequence of events, can radically alter our lifestyles.

Unfortunately, it generally takes devastation on a business level to make most men commit more of their interest in relationships. Job probably could have reached out to his children for comfort, but he had lost them too. His marriage had deteriorated to the degree that Job said his wife abhorred his breath (see Job 19:17). Then he also became ill. Have you ever gone through a time in your life when you felt you had been jinxed? Everything that could go wrong, did! Frustration turns into alienation. So now what? Will you use this moment to seek God or to brood over your misfortune? With the right answer, you could turn the jail into a church!

> *Seek ye the Lord while He may be found, call ye upon Him while He is near: let the wicked forsake his way, and the unrighteous man his thoughts: and let him return unto the Lord, and He will have mercy upon him; and to our God, for He will abundantly pardon* (Isaiah 55:6-7).

Job said, "Behold, I go forward, but He is not there" (Job 23:8a). It is terrifying when you see no change coming in the future. Comfort comes when you know that the present adversity will soon be over. But what comfort can be found when it seems the problem will never cease? Job said, "I see no help, no sign of God, in the future." It actually is satan's trick to make you think help is not coming. That hopelessness then produces anxiety. On the other hand, sometimes the feeling that you eventually will come to a point of transition can give you the tenacity to persevere the current challenge. But there often seems to be no slackening in distress. Like a rainstorm that will not cease, the waters of discouragement begin to fill the tossing ship with water. Suddenly you experience a sinking feeling. However, there is no way to sink a ship when you do not allow the waters from the outside to get on the inside! If the storms keep coming, the lightning continues to flash, and the thunder thumps on through the night, what matters is keeping the waters out of the inside. Keep that stuff out of your spirit!

Like a desperate sailor trying to plug a leaking ship, Job frantically cast back and forth in his mind, looking for some shred, some fragment of hope, to plug his leaking ship. Exasperated, he sullenly sat in the stupor of his condition and sadly confessed, "Behold, I go forward, but He is not there" (Job 23:8a). "I can't find Him where I thought He would be." Have you ever told yourself that the storm would be over soon? And the sun came and the sun left, and still the same rains beat vehemently against the ship. It almost feels as if God missed His appointment. You thought He would move by now! Glancing nervously at your watch you think, "Where is He!" Remember, dear friend, God doesn't synchronize His clock by your little mortal watch. He has a set time to bless you; just hold on.

> *For the vision is yet for an appointed time, but at the end it shall speak, and not lie: though it tarry, wait for it; because it will surely come, it will not tarry* (Habakkuk 2:3).

Someone once said that studying the past prepares us for the future. It is important to look backward and see the patterns that cause us to feel some sense of continuity. But Job said, "Looking back, I could not perceive Him" (see Job 23:8b). "Why did I have to go through all of this? Is there any reason why I had to have this struggle?" Quite honestly, there are moments when life feels like it has all the purpose of gross insanity. Like a small child cutting paper on the floor, there seems to be no real plan, only actions. These are the times that try men's hearts. These are the times when we seek answers! Sometimes, even more than change, we need answers! "God, if You don't fix it, please, please explain it!" We are reasoning people; we need to know why. Isn't that need one of the primary characteristics that separate us from animals and lesser forms of life? We are reasoning, resourceful creatures. We seek answers. Yet there are times that even after thorough evaluation, we cannot find our way out of the maze of happenstance!

Where is the God who sent an earthquake into the valley of dry bones and put them together? (See Ezekiel 37.) Or where is the God of the clay, who remolds the broken places and mends the jagged edge? (See Isaiah 64:8.) If the truth were told, the God we seek is never far away. The issue is not so much His presence as it is my perception. Many times deliverance doesn't cost God one action. Deliverance comes when my mind accepts His timing and purpose in my life.

How many persons needlessly died because they struggled in the water and finally drowned? We say they drowned because they couldn't swim. The real truth is many times they drowned because they couldn't trust! If they would relax, the same current that drummed them down would bear them up so they could float. It isn't always the circumstance that is so damaging to us; it is our reaction to the circumstance. The hysterical flailing and gasping of desperation causes us to become submerged beneath the currents of what will soon pass if we can keep our wits about us.

In my hours of crises, many times I found myself searching for the place of rest rather than for the answer. If

I can find God, I don't need to find money. If I can find God, I don't need to find healing! If I can find Him, my needs become insignificant when I wave them in the light of His presence. What is a problem if God is there? Even in the stench of Job's decaying flesh, he knew that his answer wasn't screaming out for the healing. He was screaming out for the Healer! Do you realize the power of God's presence? I hear many people speak about the acts of God, but have you ever considered the mere presence of God? He doesn't have to do anything but be there, and it is over!

If we could talk to the three Hebrews who survived the fiery furnace, perhaps they would describe their experience with the Lord in the midst of the fire in this manner:

"When we were nearing the end of the Babylonian sentencing, we knew that this would be the most trying moment of our lives. We were not sure that the Lord would deliver us, but we were sure that He was able. When they snatched us wildly from the presence of the king, the crowd was screaming hysterically, 'Burn them alive! Burn them alive!' Someone said they turned the furnace up seven times hotter than it should have been. We knew it was true for when they opened the door to throw us in, the men who threw us in were burned alive. We landed in the flames in a fright, terrified and trembling. We didn't even notice that the first miracle was our still being there.

"The fire was all over us. Our ropes were ablaze, but our skin seemed undisturbed. We didn't know what was going on. Then something moved over in the smoke and ashes. We were not alone! Out of the smoke came a shining, gleaming.... We never got His name. He never said it. He never said anything. It was His presence that brought comfort in the fire. It was His presence that created protection in the midst of the crisis. Now, we don't mean that the fire went out because He was there. No, it still burned. It was just that the burning wasn't worthy to be compared to the brilliancy of His presence. We never saw Him again. He only showed up when we needed Him most. But one thing was sure: We were glad they drug us from the presence of the wicked one into the presence of the Righteous One! In His presence we learned that, 'No weapon that is formed against thee shall prosper!'" (See Daniel 3 and Isaiah 54:17.)

Thou wilt shew me the path of life: in Thy presence is fulness of joy; at Thy right hand there are pleasures for evermore (Psalm 16:11).

No wonder Job was sitting in sackcloth and ashes searching through the rubbish of his life, looking for God. He knew that only the presence of the Lord could bring comfort to his pain! Have you begun your search for a closer manifestation of His grace? Your search alone is worship. When you seek Him, it suggests that you value Him and recognize His ability. The staggering, faulty steps of a seeker are far better than the stance of the complacent. He is not far away. He is in the furnace, moving in the ashes. Look closer. He is never far from the seeker who is on a quest to be in His presence. I don't blame the enemy for trying to convince you that you are alone. That old flame-thrower doesn't want you to find the fire-quenching presence of God!

Have you been searching and seeking and yet feel that you are getting no closer? Perhaps you are closer than you think. Here is a clue that may end your search. Job told where to find Him. He told where He works. Now if you were looking for someone and you knew where he worked, you wouldn't have to search for very long. Job said that God works on the left hand! I know you've been looking on the right hand, and I can understand why. The right hand in the Bible symbolizes power and authority. That's why Christ is seated on the right side of God (see Mark 16:19). Whenever you say someone is your right hand, you mean he is next in command or authority. *Right hand* means power. Naturally, then, if you were to search for God, you would look on the right hand. Granted, He is on the right hand. He is full of authority. But you forgot something. His strength is made perfect in weakness (see 2 Cor. 12:9). He displays His glory in the ashes of human frailty. He works on the left hand!

> *Behold, I go forward, but He is not there; and backward, but I cannot perceive Him: on the left hand, where He doth work, but I cannot behold Him; He hideth Himself on the right hand, that I cannot see Him* (Job 23:8-9).

Great growth doesn't come into your life through mountaintop experiences. Great growth comes through the valleys and low places where you feel limited and vulnerable. The time God is really moving in your life may seem to be the lowest moment you have ever experienced. Most believers think that God works when the blessing

110

comes. That's not true! God is working on you, your faith and your character, when the blessing is delayed. The blessing is the reward that comes after you learn obedience through the things you suffered while waiting for it! I wouldn't take any amount of money for the things I learned about God while I was suffering.

Now, I'm not finished suffering, and neither are you! Between every step of faith, between every new dimension of exaltation, there will always be some level of struggle. I am not finished with the left hand—nor do I want to be finished. The prerequisite of the mountain is the valley. If there is no valley, there is no mountain. After you've been through this process a few times, you begin to realize that the valley is only a sign that with a few more steps, you'll be at the mountain again! Thus if the left hand is where He works, and it is; if the left hand is where He teaches us, and it is; then at the end of every class is a promotion. So just hold on!

However, there is one final issue needing discussion. It is difficult to perceive God's workings on the left hand. God makes definite moves on the right hand, but when He works on the left, you may think He has forgotten you! If you've been living on the left side, you've been through a period that didn't seem to have the slightest stirring. It seemed as if everything you wanted to see God move upon, stayed still. "Has He gone on vacation? Has He forgotten His promise?" you've asked. The answer is no! God hasn't forgotten. You simply need to understand that sometimes He moves openly. I call them right-hand blessings.

But sometimes He moves silently, tip-toeing around in the invisible, working in the shadows. You can't see Him, for He is working on the left side!

Let me present my daughter Cora as an illustration. When she was born, her mother and I noticed that she learned to hold her bottle in her right hand. We naturally assumed that she was right-handed. However, to our surprise, when she grew a little older she held her cup in her left hand. To this day there are certain things she does with her right hand and certain things she does with her left. Technically, they call it ambidexterity. Cora is what my grandmother would call even-handed. The hand she uses depends on what she is trying to accomplish. Cora is ambidextrous. So is God! He is simply ambidextrous. There are times He will move on the left side.

Listen for God's hammering in the spirit. You can't see Him when He's working on the left side; He is invisible over there. It appears that He is not there, but He is.

I feel by the Holy Spirit that somewhere there is a reader whom God wants to make sure this principle gets in his spirit. You have been going through a time of left-side experiences. You've said over and over again, "Where is the move of God that I used to experience? Why am I going through these fiery trials?" Let me minister to you a minute. God is there with you even now. He is operating in a different realm. He is working with a different hand, but He is still working in your life! In order for Him to do this job in your life, He had to change hands. Trust Him to have the same level of dexterity in His left hand as He does when He moves with the right hand.

I know so well how hard it is to trust Him when you can't trace Him! But that's exactly what He wants you to do—He wants you to trust Him with either hand. It may seem that everybody is passing you right now. Avoid measuring yourself against other people. God knows when the time is right. His methods may seem crude and His teachings laborious, but His results will be simply breathtaking. Without scams and games, without trickery or politics, God will accomplish a supernatural miracle because you trusted Him while He worked on the left side.

How long does God work on the left? I don't know. It's like the phrase, "Different strokes for different folks." I will tell you one thing, though; Job concluded that God knows the way he takes. That means even when I didn't know where He was, He always knew where I was. God has never taken His eye off you, and He knows where you are every minute. Furthermore, Job said, "When He hath tried me..." (Job 23:10b). The word when makes me want to shout because it implies that God has a set time for my going through the test and a set time for bringing me out. Then I'm happy also because it's He who is trying me, not my enemies. It's not the devil, but God! I wouldn't trust anybody else but Him to take me through these left-side experiences. He loves me enough to give me everything I need to live with Him on the left side. To those who have no might He increases strength. New mercies come forth when you fight old problems!

I've learned to be thankful for the end results. Through every test and trial you must tell yourself what

Job said. "I shall come forth as pure gold. I might not come forth today. It might not even be tomorrow. But when God gets through melting out all the impurities and scraping off the dross; when the boiling and the toilings of trouble have receded and the liquified substances in my life have become stable and fixed, then I will shine!" You bubbling, tempestuous saint who is enduring a time of walking through the left side of God, be strong and very courageous. The process always precedes the promise!

Soon you will be reshaped and remade into a gold chalice from which only the King can drink. All dross is discarded; all fear is removed. The spectators will gather to ask how such a wonderful vessel was made out of such poor materials. They will behold the jewels of your testimony and the brilliant glory of that fresh anointing. Some will wonder if you are the same person that they used to know. How do you answer? Simply stated, just say no!

Now you sit on the Master's right side, ready and available to be used, a vessel of honor unto Him. No matter how glorious it is to sit on His right hand and be brought to a position of power, just remember that although you have overcome now, you were boiled down and hollowed out while you lived on the left side of God. Join me in looking back over your life. Review your left-side experiences. Taste the bitter tears and the cold winds of human indifference and never, ever let anyone make you forget. You and I know. It's our secret, whether we tell them or sit quietly and make small talk. You've not always been where you are or shined as you shine. What can I say? You've come a long way, baby!

Chapter 9

A SURVIVAL COURSE
FOR SMALL BEGINNINGS

For who hath despised the day of small things? for they shall rejoice, and shall see the plummet in the hand... (Zechariah 4:10).

Why do so many people try to convey the image that they have always been on top? The truth is most people have struggled to attain whatever they have. They just try to convince everyone that they have always had it. I, for one, am far more impressed with the wealth of a person's character who doesn't use his success to intimidate others. The real, rich inner stability that comes from gradual success is far more lasting and beneficial than the temperamental theatrics of spiritual yuppies who have never learned their own vulnerabilities. We must not take ourselves too seriously. I believe that God grooms us for greatness in the stockades of struggle.

I remember so well the early struggles that my wife and I had to maintain our family, finances, and overall well-being while building a ministry. I was working a secular job that God wanted me to leave for full-time ministry. Full-time ministry—what a joke! I was scarcely asked to preach anywhere that offered more than a few pound cakes, a couple jars of jelly, and if I was lucky, enough gas money to get home. My hotel generally would be the back room of some dear elderly church mother who charmingly entertained me as best she could with what she had. It was there, around old coal stoves in tiny churches that never even considered buying a microphone, that I learned how to preach. Often I would preach until sweaty and tired, to rows of empty pews with two or three people who decorated the otherwise empty church like earrings placed on the head of a bald doll.

Finally I said yes to full-time ministry. I did it not because I wanted it, but because the company I worked for went out of business and I was forced out of my comfort zone into the land of faith. What a frightening experience it was to find myself without. "Without what?" you ask. I was without everything you could think of: without a job and then a car. Later I was without utilities and often without food. I scraped around doing odd jobs trying to feed two children and a wife without looking like life wasn't working. I thought God had forgotten me. I even preached in suits that shined. They shined not because they were in style, but because they were worn, pressed with an iron, and eventually washed in the washing machine because cleaners were out of the question. I am not ashamed to tell you—in fact I am proud to tell you—that I experienced more about God in those desperate days of struggle as I answered the charges of satan with the perseverance of prayer.

> *Then Satan answered the Lord, and said, Doth Job fear God for nought? Hast not Thou made an hedge about him, and about his house, and about all that he hath on every side? Thou hast blessed the work of his hands, and his substance is increased in the land. But put forth Thine hand now, and touch all that he hath, and he will curse Thee to Thy face* (Job 1:9-11).

Satan cannot dispute your serving God, but he challenges our reason for serving Him. He says it is for the prominence and protection that God provides. He further insinuates that if things weren't going so well, we would not praise God so fervently. The devil is a liar! In each of our lives, in one way or another, we will face times when we must answer satan's charges and prove that even in the storm, He is still God!

Those early times of challenge sorely tried all that was in me. My pride, my self-esteem, and my self-confidence teetered like a child learning to ride a bicycle. My greatest fear was that it would never end. I feared that, like a person stuck in an elevator, I would spend the rest of my life between floors—neither here nor there in an intermediate stage of transition. I felt like a shoulder out of joint and in pain.

I learned, however, that if you can remember your beginnings and still reach toward your goals, God will bless you with things without fear of those items becoming idols in your life. Oddly, there is a glory in the agonizing of early years that people who didn't have to struggle seem not to possess. There is a strange sense of competence that comes from being born in the flames of struggle. How wildly exuberant are the first steps of the child who earlier was mobile only through crawling on his hands and knees.

> *According to the grace of God which is given unto me, as a wise masterbuilder, I have laid the foundation, and another buildeth thereon. But let every man take heed how he buildeth thereupon. For other foundation can no man lay than that is laid, which is Jesus Christ* (1 Corinthians 3:10-11).

I have found God to be a builder of men. When He builds, He emphasizes the foundation. A foundation, once it is laid, is neither visible nor attractive, but nevertheless still quite necessary. When God begins to establish the foundation, He does it in the feeble, frail beginnings of our lives. Paul describes himself as a wise master builder. Actually, God is the Master Builder. He knows what kind of beginning we need and He lays His foundation in the struggles of our formative years.

The concern over the future coupled with the fear of failure brings us to the posture of prayer. I don't think I completely realized how severe those early years were because I saw them through the tinted glasses of grace. I had been gifted with the grace to endure. Often we don't realize how severe our beginnings were until we are out or about to come out of them. Then the grace lifts and we behold the utter devastating truth about what we just came through.

When I was very small, my family had a tradition we observed every Sunday breakfast. Every Sunday morning my mother would go into the kitchen while we were still asleep and begin making homemade waffles for breakfast. These were real waffles. I don't remember all the ingredients she had in them, but I do remember that this particular recipe required beating the egg whites and then folding them into the waffle batter. These waffles were very light and their texture hasn't been seen since the *Ted Mack Hour* hosted the Beatles for their first debut.

When I would rise, clad in a pair of worn pajamas and scuffy shoes, the smell of waffles would fill the room with the kind of aroma that made you float out of the bed. I can still see that old waffle iron. It was round and had an old cord that was thick and striped. On the top of the shiny round lid was a thermostat that showed how hot the waffles were. My mother never needed it because the waffle would begin to steam and hiss. It would push that lid up as if the waffle had been sleeping too and decided to rise. There was no doubt in anybody's mind that they were done. They smelled like Hallelujah and they looked like glory to God—if you know what I mean. They took a long time to prepare, but these waffles took your mouth to the butter-filled streams of heaven. Breakfast on Sunday morning was a religious experience.

The other day I tasted some of these modern carbon-copy, freezer burned, cardboard-clad waffles. My taste buds recoiled. Those things should be arrested for impersonating

a waffle. I am convinced that most of the following generations will never know the soft, succulent experience of
sticking a clean fork into the butter-filled, syrup-drenched,
angel-light waffles that I grew up on. These instant waffles
that leap out of a toaster like Houdini have about all the
tender texture of rawhide. My point is, I am afraid that too
many Christians pop off the altar like these cardboard
waffles. They are overnight wonders. They are 24-hour
pastors with a Bible they haven't read and a briefcase
more valuable than the sermons in it!

I know this sounds old-fashioned, but I believe anything worth doing is worth doing well. God Himself takes
His time developing us. No instant success will do. He
wants to put the quality in before the name goes out. A
small beginning is just the prelude to a tremendous
crescendo at the finale! Many of God's masterpieces were
developed in small obscure circumstances. Moses, the
messiah of the Old Testament sent to the lost sheep of
Israel, was trained in leadership while shoveling sheep
dung on the backside of the desert. There was no fancy
finishing school for this boy. Granted, his discipline was
developed in the royal courts of Pharaoh's house, but his
disposition was shaped through a failure in his life and a
desert kingdom with no one to lead but flies, gnats, and
sheep. Who would have thought, looking at Moses'
church of goat deacons and gnats for choir members, that
he later would lead the greatest movement in the history
of Old Testament theology?

Who would have guessed that old impotent Abraham, whose sun had gone down and force gone out,

would finally father a nation—in fact, a nationality? One moment he is sitting on the edge of the bed with an embarrassed look on his face and the next moment he is fathering children even after Sarah's death. You can't tell what's in you by looking at you. God is establishing patience, character, and concentration in the school of "nothing seems to be happening." Take the class and get the course credit; it's working for your good.

Many misunderstand the prophecies of the Lord and so feel discontentment and despair. Just because God promises to move in your life and anoints you to do a particular function doesn't mean that your foundation will be immediately built. Directly after David was anointed to lead Israel, he was sent back into the field to feed the sheep. Joseph received a dream from the Lord that showed him ruling and reigning over his brothers, but in the next event his brothers stripped him, beat him, and tossed him in a hole. Can you imagine what the devil said to Joseph while he nursed his scrapes and bruises in the dark hole of small beginnings?

Swallowed up with bruises and scars, he listened to the sound of depression sweeping through his throbbing head that beat like the congo drums of an African warrior. Satan's laugh filled the dark channels of the hole with his evil hysteria. "So you were going to reign, were you? I thought the dream said you were in charge," the enemy taunted. Satan didn't understand that all great prophecies start out small. Like chestnuts in the hand of a child, those same chestnuts will one day be large enough to hold a child like the one who once held them. God has not changed His mind. His methods may seem crude, but His purpose is to provide wonderful success. Don't die in the hole! God hasn't changed His mind. He is a Master Builder and He spends extra time laying a great foundation.

When the first man Adam was created, he was created full grown. He had no childhood, no small things. He was just immediately a man. But when it was time for the last man Adam, God didn't create Him full grown. No, He took His time and laid a foundation. He was born a child and laid in a manger. The Manager of the universe was laid in a manger. "For unto us a child is born, unto us a son is given..." (Isa. 9:6). The Bible says that He grew in favor with God and man (see Luke 2:52). Not too fast, but He grew. Please allow yourself time to grow.

Once I was praying for the Lord to move mightily in my ministry. I had asked, fasted, and prayed. I had probably begged a little and foamed at the mouth too, but none of it hurried the plan of God in my life. After many days of absolute silence, He finally sent me a little answer. The Lord answered my prayer by saying, "You are concerned about building a ministry, but I am concerned about building a man." He concluded by mentioning this warning, which has echoed in my ears all of my life. He said, "Woe unto the man whose ministry becomes bigger than he is!" Since then I have concerned myself with praying for the minister and not for the ministry. I realized that if the house outgrows the foundation, gradually the foundation will crack, the walls will collapse, and great will be the fall of it!

No matter what you are trying to build, whether it is a business, a ministry, or a relationship, give it time to grow. Some of the best friendships start out gradually. Some of the strongest Christians once desperately needed prayer for their weaknesses. I am still amazed at who I am becoming as I put my life daily into His hands. He is changing me. He's not finished. There is so much more that needs to be done. Every day I see more immaturity in me. But, what a sharp contrast I am now to what I was.

Humility is a necessity when you know that every accomplishment had to be the result of the wise Master Builder who knows when to do what. He knew when I needed friends. He knew when I needed to sit silently in the night, wrap my arms around my limitations, and whisper a soft request for help into the abyss of my pain. He is the One who rolls back the clouds on the storms and orders the rain to stop. Oh, how I trust Him more dearly and more nearly than I have ever trusted Him before. He is too wise to make a mistake!

If you are praying, "Lord, make me bigger," you are probably miserable, although prayerful. Did you know you can be prayerful and still be miserable? Anytime you use prayer to change God, who is perfect, instead of using prayer to change yourself, you are miserable. Stop manipulating God! Stop trying to learn something you can say to God to make Him do what He knows you are not ready to endure or receive. Instead, try praying this: "Lord, make me better." I admit that better is harder to measure and not as noticeable to the eye. But better will overcome bigger every time.

What a joy it is to be at peace with who you are and where you are in your life. How restful it is to not try and beat the clock with friends or try to prove anything to foes. You will never change their minds anyway, so change your own. I want to be better—to have a better character, better confidence, and a better attitude! The desire to be bigger will not allow you to rest, relax, or enjoy your blessing. The desire to be better, however, will afford you a barefoot stroll down a deserted beach. You can sit in the sand, throw shells into the water, and shiver when the tide rushes up too high. Sing into the wind a song out of tune. It may not harmonize, but it will be full of therapy. There are probably many things you didn't get done and so much you have left to do. But isn't it nice to sigh, relax, and just thank God for the things—the little, tiny, small things—that you know He brought you through. Thank God for small things.

Chapter 10

CAN YOU STAND TO BE BLESSED?

The obscure side of a struggle is the awesome wrestling match many people have with success. First success is given only at the end of great struggle. If it were easy, anybody could do it. Success is success only because it relates to struggle. How can you have victory without conflict? To receive something without struggle lessens its personal value. Success is the reward that God gives to the diligent who, through perseverance, obtain the promise. There is no way to receive what God has for your life without fighting the obstacles and challenges that block your way to conquest. In fact, people who procrastinate do so because they are desperately trying to find a way to reach the goal without going through the struggle.

When I was a youngster, we kids used to go into the stores and change the price tags on the items we could not afford. We weren't stealing, we thought, because we did pay something. It just wasn't nearly what the vendor wanted us to pay. I guess we thought we would put the product on sale without the permission of the store manager. I believe many people are trying to do the same thing today in their spiritual life. They are attempting to get a discount on the promises of God. That doesn't work in the Kingdom. Whatever it costs, it costs; there is no swapping the price tags.

You must pay your own way. Your payment helps you to appreciate the blessings when they come because you know the expense. You will not easily jeopardize the welfare of something not easily attained.

The zeal it takes to be effective at accomplishing a goal ushers you up the steps of life. As you journey up the steps, it becomes increasingly difficult to be successful without others finding you offensive. Some people will find your success offensive, whether or not you are arrogant. They are offended at what God does for you. I call those people "Cain's children." Cain's children, like their father, will murder you because you have God's favor. Watch out for them. They will not rejoice with you. They can't be glad for you because somehow they feel your success came at their expense. They foolishly believe that you have their blessing. No diplomacy can calm a jealous heart. They don't want to pay what you paid, but they want to have what you have.

> *And the Lord said unto Cain, Why art thou wroth? and why is thy countenance fallen? If thou doest well, shalt thou not be accepted? and if thou doest not well, sin lieth at the door...* (Genesis 4:6-7).

It is amazing the relationships that can be lost as you travel upward. As long as you're in the day of small beginnings, you are acceptable. If you accelerate into new dimensions, however, cynicism eats at the fibers of their conversations and in their hearts. Cain's children will invite you into their field to destroy you. Must you then be defensive? How can you defend yourself from another person's reaction to you? Then you become imprisoned by paranoia. It is difficult to be careful without being distrustful and cynical. "Are we not brothers?" Sure we are. Yet Jesus said, "And a man's foes shall be they of his own household" (Matt. 10:36). Your enemy will not wound you because he is too far way. In order to be a good Judas, he must be at the table with the victim of his betrayal! Who sits at your table?

Imagine Jesus, at the height of His ministerial career, sitting at the table with John, the beloved, on one side and Judas, the betrayer, on the other. The problem is in discerning which one is which. One of them is close enough to lay his head on your breast. The other has enough access to you to betray you with a kiss. They are both intimate, but one is lethal. Yet, in the midst of this harsh and rather bleak panoramic view of success, you must depend on the Lord to keep whatever He commits into your hands, at least until His purpose is accomplished. Keep your affections on the Giver and not the gifts. "Lord, help us to keep our eyes on the things that will not change."

There also is the fact that the more you have or own, the more you are responsible for. People who have no car need no gas. With every blessing there is an additional responsibility. How many times have you prayed for a blessing? Then, when you received it, you realized there were strings attached that you didn't originally consider? To be honest, being blessed is hard work. Everything God gives you requires maintenance. God gave man the Garden, but the man still had to dress it. There is a "down" side to every blessing. That is why Jesus said, "No man builds without counting the cost" (see Lk. 14:28-30). You must ask yourself if you are willing to pay the price to get the blessing. Another question people seldom ask themselves is whether they are willing to endure the criticism and the ridicule that come with success.

With these questions we have already weeded out half the people who say they want something from the Lord. We have weeded out all the women who say they want a husband and children but don't want to cook, care, or clean. We have weeded out all the men who say they want a wife but don't want to love, provide, and nourish! Most people are in love with the image of success, but they haven't contemplated the reality of possessing the blessing. It is a good thing God doesn't give us everything we ask for because we want some things simply because they look good in someone else's life. The truth is, we are not ready for those things and it would probably kill us to receive what we are not prepared to maintain.

His lord said unto him, Well done, good and faithful servant; thou hast been faithful over a few things, I will make thee ruler over many things: enter thou into the joy of thy lord (Matthew 25:23).

So you're whimsically toying with the idea of exercising your ability to receive a blessing? This is a good place to start. I believe that God starts His children out with what they have to teach consistency on the level they are on. There must be an inner growth in your ability to withstand the struggles that accompany the things you have. I am so glad that God allowed me to go through the pain-ridden days of stress and rejection early in my life. I found out that if you really want to pursue your dream, there is a place in God whereby you build up an immunity to the adversity of success. It is simply a matter of survival. Either you become immune to the criticism and confusing pressures and isolation, or you go absolutely stark raving, mouth-foaming mad!

If you are always weeping over rejection and misunderstanding, if you're always upset over who doesn't accept you into their circles anymore, you may be suffering from an immunity deficiency syndrome. You waste precious time of communion when you ask God to change the minds of people. It is not the people or the pressure that must change, it is you. In order to survive the stresses of success, you must build up an immunity to those things that won't change. Thank God that He provides elasticity for us. Remember, you can't switch price tags just because you don't like the price. My constant prayer is, "Lord, change me until this doesn't hurt anymore." I am like David—I am forever praying my way into the secret place. The secret place in the king's court was called a pavilion. There you are insulated from the enemy. If you could make it to the secret place, all hell could break loose outside, but it would not matter to you, for in the secret place is peace. If you want to accomplish much, if you intend to survive Cain's hateful children, then you need to get in the secret place and stay there!

> *For in the time of trouble He shall hide me in His pavilion: in the secret of His tabernacle shall He hide me; He shall set me up upon a rock* (Psalm 27:5).

What a place of solace God has for the weary heart who is bombarded with the criticism of cynical people and the pressures to perform. I often think of how many times I allowed to overwhelm me things that really didn't make any difference. In retrospect, half of the things I was praying about should have been dismissed as trivialities. Maturity is sweet relief for the person who hasn't yet learned how to survive the blessings God has given them. I know that sounds strange, but many people don't survive their own success. Notoriety comes and goes, but when it is over you want to still be around. Many people lose their own identities in the excitement of the moment. When the excitement ebbs, as it always does, they have lost sight of the more important issues of self, home, and family!

Another issue is your change in values as you progress. Hopefully your morality does not change, but your sense of what is and is not acceptable should. For example, consider how differently you feel now as opposed to how you felt when you were younger. When I was younger, something six or eight blocks away was right around the corner. Today I can still walk as far as I did then, I am just not sure that I want to. In the same way, luxuries become necessities once you become accustomed to them. Once you are exposed to certain things, it is difficult to go back to what other people might consider normal. If that's not true, then why don't you stir cake batter with a spoon like my mother did when I was small? I can still see her arm beating and beating the butter into the sugar. Who wants to do that now?

Why don't people wash their clothes on a washboard like my grandmother did? She used to boil the white clothes in a pot and then hang them in the sun. As for bleach, what was that? When the microwave was first introduced, consumers were afraid of it. Now you can't imagine not having one. My point should be obvious. Once you become accustomed to any lifestyle, it is hard to go back to what you once thought was sufficient. To add to the complexity of this issue, when you move into a different place in your life, you are still surrounded by people in the other stage. Now you must deal with envy and criticism. Many people suffer inside because they are surrounded by others who live where they were and not where they are. These are the same type of people who called Christ the carpenter's son (see Matt. 13:55).

Dear friend, as painful as it is to be criticized by those you are in covenant with, it is far worse to give up the course that God has for you just for their acceptance. In short, as much as you need to be affirmed and understood, at some point you must ask yourself, "How much am I willing to lose in order to be accepted?" If the truth were told, people do not always want to see you move on—especially if they perceive you as moving more rapidly than they are. Can you endure the pressure they will put on you to come down? Or will you be like Nehemiah, who said, "I am doing a great work, so that I cannot come down" (Neh. 6:3b). Exaltation may cost you a degree of acceptance and reward you with isolation. In fact, God may be grooming you right now for a new level by exposing you to opposition and criticism. He may be building up your immunity so when the greater blessing comes, you won't break.

Successful people tend to be passionate people. These are people who have intense desire. I admit there are many passionate people who are not successful. But I didn't say that passionate people are successful; I said that successful people tend to be passionate. You can be passionate and not be successful. Passion, basically, is raw power. If it is not harnessed and focused for a goal, it becomes an animalistic force. But if you can focus passion for a divine purpose, you will be successful. Some people never use their desire in a positive way. Instead of harnessing it and allowing it to become the force they use to overcome hindrances, it becomes a source of frustration and cynicism. Success only comes to a person who is committed to a cause or has a passion to achieve. The crux of the matter basically is this: "How bad do you want to be blessed?"

How strong is your desire for accomplishment in your life? It takes more than a mere whimsical musing over a speculative end. It takes floor-walking, devil-stomping, anointed tenacity to overcome the limitations that are always surrounding what you want to do for your God, yourself, and your family! If you don't have sufficient passion, you will never have the force to overcome limitations and satanic restrictions. Power emerges from the heart of a man who is relentlessly driven toward a goal. Desire is kindled in the furnace of need—an unfulfilled need. It is a need that refuses to be placated and a need that will not be silent. Any man will tell you that where there is no desire, there is no passion. Where there is no passion, there is no potency. Without desire, you are basically impotent!

Desire gives you the drive you need to produce. Even natural reproduction is an impossibility to a person who is devoid of passion and desire. Many people who set out to accomplish goals are so easily discouraged or intimidated by their own anxieties that they relinquish their right to fight for their dreams. However, if there is a tenacious burning desire in the pit of your stomach, you become very difficult to discourage. How many cold nights I have warmed my cold feet by the fires of my innermost desire to complete a goal for my life. No one knows how hot the embers glow beneath the ashes of adversity.

Having pastored in the coal fields of West Virginia, I know about wood and coal stoves. You can bank the fire by placing ashes all around it. Then it will not burn out as rapidly and will last through the night. In the frosty chill of the morning you do not need to rebuild the fire, for beneath the ashes lay crimson embers waiting to be stirred. These embers explode into a fire when they are stirred correctly. Many people have gone through situations that banked their fire. The fire isn't dead, but its burning is not as brilliant as it once was. I am glad that if you have an inner desire to survive or succeed, then you only need a stirring for the embers of passion to ignite in your life.

I love to surround myself with people who can stir up the fire in me. Some people in the Body of Christ know just what to say to ignite the very fire in you. However, no one can ignite in you what you do not possess! If the cold winds of opposition have banked the fire and your dream is dying down, I challenge you to rekindle your desire to achieve whatever God has called you to do. Don't lose your fire. You need that continued spark for excellence to overcome all the blight of being ostracized.

Fire manifests itself in two ways. First, it gives light. Whenever you maintain your fire, it produces the light of optimism against the blackness of crises and critics alike. As long as you maintain that firelike attitude, you will find a way to survive the struggle. A man never dies with a twinkle in his eyes. Second, fire gives heat. Heat can't be seen, but it can be felt. When you are burning with the passion to survive, the heat can be felt. Invisible but effective, your intensity is always detected in your speech and attitude.

Every man and woman of God must also remember that fire needs fuel. Feed the fire. Feed it with the words of people who motivate you. Feed it with vision and purpose. When stress comes, fan the flames. Gather the wood. Pour gasoline if you have to, but don't let it die!

Sometimes just seeing God bless someone else gives you the fortitude to put a demand on the promise that God has given you. I don't mean envy, but a strong provocation to receive. Look at the situation of Hannah, Elkanah's wife, in First Samuel 1. She wanted to have a child. In order to stir up Hannah, God used a girl named Peninnah who was married to the same man but able to bear children. The more Hannah saw Peninnah have children, the more she desired her own. Peninnah provoked Hannah; she stirred Hannah's embers. She made Hannah pray. It wasn't that Hannah got jealous and didn't want to see Peninnah be blessed. She didn't begrudge the other woman her blessing. She just wanted her own. If seeing others blessed makes you want to sabotage their success, then you will not be fruitful. I have learned how to rejoice over the blessings of my brother and realize that the same God who blessed him can bless me also. Other people's blessings ought to challenge you to see that it can be done.

Success cannot be defined in generalities; it can be defined only according to individual purpose and divine direction. If you don't understand this concept, you can have great riches or fame and still be unsuccessful. You would be surprised at how many highly anointed people are tormented by a need to evaluate themselves in the light of another's calling. Your assignment is to dig for your own gold. Just cultivate what the Lord has given to you. It's simple: Find out what you have to work with, and then work it, work it, work it!

I am always concerned that Christians not manipulate each other by trying to get people to worship their talents rather than God's purpose for their lives. How can any person know you well enough to discern whether you are successful, other than the God who created you? In short, there is no way to define success without examining purpose. What did the inventor have in mind when he made the machine? That is the first question. The second question asks, "Did it accomplish the purpose it was created to perform?" It doesn't matter what else it did; if it didn't satisfy the mandate of its creator, it is unsuccessful. When people other than the Creator define success, it becomes idolatry. Some people would have you worship at the shrine of their accomplishments. Of course you should appreciate and encourage them, but don't be manipulated by them. Suppose your heart told your kidneys, "Unless you pump blood, you are not successful." Never mind that the kidneys purify the blood that the heart pumps. It would be foolish for the kidneys to believe that statement. It would shut down the whole body! That's what happens when we, as the Body, fail to maintain our individuality!

> *...For unto whomsoever much is given, of him shall be much required: and to whom men have committed much, of him they will ask the more* (Luke 12:48).

There are no ifs, ands, or buts; the greater the blessing, the more the responsibility. It is expensive to be blessed. Everyone can't handle the success. Some may choose tranquillity over notoriety. They don't like criticism and they abhor pressure. But if you are the kind of person who desperately needs to attain the hope of his calling, then go for it. Some people will never be satisfied with sitting on the bench cheering for others who paid the price to play the game. Locked within them is an inner ambitious intrigue not predicated on jealousy or intimidation. It is built upon an inner need to unlock a predestined purpose. For them, it does not matter. Inflationary times may escalate the price of their dreams, but whatever the price, they are compelled, drawn, and almost driven toward a hope.

Many people are drawn toward their destiny with such a force and an attraction that regardless of what it takes, what they must readjust, or what they must discipline, they simply must respond to life's challenges. Neither lethal nor dangerous, they merely move aggressively toward purpose. For myself, I am not afraid of dying; I am not afraid of leaving as much as I am afraid of not living first. What absolutely terrifies me is the thought that I would stand beside life like a miser who longs for a certain article but is too crippled by his incessant fear of expense to buy. If you want it, pay the price.

I confess, I have cried huge salty tears. I have felt the bitter pangs of rejection and criticism. I admit there were times that I rocked my worries to sleep in the middle of the night. Know all this and understand that I have not yet seen a day that made me regret the decision to run my course. How far or how fast you run in comparison with others doesn't matter. Whether you win trophies or receive great accolades doesn't matter. What matters is that you stretch your legs and run in the wind. It is only your shadow that you run against. It is your own destiny that you stride beside.

I am told that distance runners make long, steady strides and that their emphasis is on endurance, not speed. They take their laps and stretch their limitations, giving themselves over to committing their strength to a goal. Perspiration leaps out of their pores. The salty taste of exertion is in their mouths. Turning corners with agility, running shoes banging the pavement, heads high, backs straight—they are in pursuit of a goal. I am told that as they near the finish line, there is a final burst of energy that kicks in like the final cylinders in an engine. It is the last lap; there are no excuses; it's now or never. Now they go for broke! At least once, before they roll you in on a slab and put a name tag on your cold stiff toe, you owe it to your God and to yourself to experience in some area in your life that last-lap feeling of giving your all.

I want to warn you, though, that it hurts to push yourself. It is not easy to get up early every morning while others sleep and prepare for the challenge. Like Jesus in the garden of Gethsemane, it is difficult to find someone who will stand with you while you are in preparation. But there can be no celebration without preparation.

Before we end this issue, there are some truths I would like to underscore. First, huge stress comes with success in any area. Before you ask for the house, be sure you have counted up the cost. If, after you calculate the rejection, controversy, criticism, and isolation, you still want it, then realize that you cannot stand the pain of a cross unless you have before you something more important than the pain you endure in the process.

For many of us there is no option. We must go to the pinnacle of our own purpose, stand on the top of the mountain, and catch a glimpse of the other side. We are climbing up the mountain with tears in our eyes and dirt in our fingernails. In spite of bruises, cuts, and scrapes, there is a racing pulse and a pounding heart that exist in the chest of someone who has made up his mind, "I will go!"

CAN YOU STAND TO BE BLESSED?

The question is universal but the answer is totally individual. Can *you* stand to be blessed? If you answer yes, then I want to tell you this: The only way to be blessed is to stand! When you can't seem to put one foot in front of the other, stand. When days come that challenge your destiny, just stand. Realize that there has never been a day that lasted forever. You can't afford to crumple onto your knees like a weak, whimpering lily blown over by a windstorm. Bite your lip, taste your tears, but stand on what God showed you in the night until it happens in the light.

Chapter 11

RETURN TO SENDER

There must be something beyond the acquisition of a goal. If there isn't, then this book is nothing more than a motivational message, something which the secular field is already adept at. Many people spend all their lives trying to attain a goal. When they finally achieve it, they still secretly feel empty and unfulfilled. This will happen even in the pursuit of godly goals and successes if we don't reach beyond the mere accomplishment of an ambitious pursuit. In short, success doesn't save! Why then does God put the desire to attain in the hearts of His men and women if He knows that at the end is, as Solomon so aptly put it, "Vanity of vanities...all is vanity" (Eccles. 12:8)? Could it be that we who have achieved something of effectiveness must then reach a turn in the road and begin to worship God beyond the goal!

A runner trains himself to achieve a goal. That goal ultimately is to break the ribbon, the mark of success. After he has broken the ribbon, if there is no prize beyond the goal, then the race seems in vain. No runner would run a race and then receive the broken ribbon as the symbol of his success. At the end of the race is a prize unrelated to the race itself—a trophy that can be given only to people who have reached the pinnacle of accomplishment. What we must understand in the back of our minds as we ascend toward God's purpose is it blesses God when we attain what we were created to attain. It is His eternal purpose that we pursue. However, we can be blessed only by the God behind the purpose. If we build a great cathedral for the Lord and fail to touch the God whom the cathedral is for, what good is the building aside from God?

Why are we always such extremists? Some of us spend all our lives doing absolutely nothing for the Lord. We are constantly in His presence, praising His name, but we fail to accomplish anything relative to His purpose. Isaiah was in the presence of God to such a degree that the glory of the Lord filled the temple like a train, and the doorpost moved (see Isa. 6:1-4). Nevertheless, there was still a time when God sent him from His presence to accomplish His purpose. As an eagle stirs her nest, so God must challenge us to leave the familiar places and perform the uncertain future of putting into practice the total of all we have learned in the Lord's presence. The priest went into the Holy of Holies to see the glory of the Lord, but the work of the Lord was to be performed outside the veiled place of secret consecration. As Isaiah said, "Here am I; send me" (Isa. 6:8), go from the gluttony of storing up the treasure to being a vessel God can use!

The other extreme is equally, if not more, dangerous. What makes us think we can do the work of the Lord and never spend time with the Lord of the work? We get burned out when we do not keep fresh fire burning within! We need the kind of fire that comes from putting down all the work and saying to the Lord, "I need my time with You." What good is it to break the finish line if you do not go beyond that temporary moment of self-aggrandizement to receive a valued reward? The accomplishment isn't reward enough because once it is attained, it ceases to be alluring.

For example, when my twin boys were toddlers, I helped potty train them. When they learned to use the potty, we had an all-out celebration. I never knew I could be that glad to see a bowel movement in a pot! However ridiculous as it might sound, we all clamorously screamed and laughed and were delighted at this moment of success. They are now 14 years old. We don't quite act that way now when necessity mandates that they visit the toilet. We do not continue to celebrate what we have already accomplished.

Since the beauty of the moment soon fades and you find yourself again seeking new conquest, there must be something beyond just achieving goals and setting new goals. You would be surprised at the number of pastors all across this country who race wildly from one goal to the other without ever feeling fulfilled by their accomplishments. What is even worse is the fact that other men and women often envy and sometimes hate these ministers because they would love to have what these ministers have attained. Yet the poor chaps themselves can't see their own worth. Little does anyone know that these spiritual celebrities are being widely driven by the need to accomplish without ever being fulfilled. It is the cruelest form of torture to be secretly dying of the success which others envy. If you are in that situation, whether you are a business person or a minister, I speak to your addiction (that's right, addiction) in the name of Jesus Christ. I command that nagging, craving, family-abusing ambition to loose you and let you go!

Release comes so you can enter the presence of God to be restored. To be restored means to be built back up, to be restocked. Only God can put back into you what striving took out. Will you strive for a goal again? Yes! You need to strive, but you don't need the obsession that it can create. There will never be anything that God gives you to do that will replace what God's mere presence will give. You will never build your self-esteem by accomplishing goals because, as in the case of my twins, once you've done it, it's done! No lasting affirmation comes from a mountain that has been climbed. Only Christ can save you, affirm you, and speak to how you feel about yourself. The praises of men will fall into the abyss of a leaky heart. When you have a crack, everything in you will leak out. Let God fix it. Your job can't do it. Sex can't do it. Marriage can't do it. Another graduate degree can't do it, but God can! He is the Doctor who specialized in reconstructive surgery!

The four and twenty elders fall down before Him that sat on the throne, and worship Him that liveth for ever and ever, and cast their crowns before the throne,

144

saying, Thou art worthy, O Lord, to receive glory and honour and power: for Thou hast created all things, and for Thy pleasure they are and were created (Revelation 4:10-11).

There is a place in the presence of God where crowns lose their luster. There is a place where the accolades of men sound brash and out of pitch. There is a place where all our memorials of great accomplishments seem like dusty stones gathered by bored children who had nothing better to collect. There are times when we trade success for solace. In Revelation, 24 elders traded their golden, jewel-encrusted crowns for a tear-stained moment in the presence of a blood-stained Lamb. Many wonderful people are suffering with their success because they cannot discern when to throw down their crowns and just worship.

Have you ever driven a vehicle that had a stick shift? I have. I drove a delivery truck one summer while I was in college. I had never driven a stick shift vehicle before. It was all right at first. I handled it rather well. In fact, I was on my way to that special place of self-enthroned egotism when I had to stop at a traffic light. The only problem was, this light was on a steep hill. Suddenly my confidence turned to the acidic taste of gastric juices pushing up through my esophagus. I had to keep my left foot on the clutch while easing my right foot from the brake to the gas with the timing and grace of Fred Astaire. My first attempt caused the truck to lurch forward, when the engine died and the whole truck started sliding backwards. I nearly slid into a car that was behind me. I was sick! Traffic was backing up and I could see the person in my rearview mirror saying something that I was glad I couldn't quite hear!

After a few more failed attempts at being an auto-ballerina, I calmed myself, trying to ignore the cars that were whirling around me and the drivers making gestures that even a blind person could interpret. I finally prayed—which is what I should have done at first. My task was getting the timing. I had to learn when to ease my right foot off the brake and onto the gas and my left foot from the clutch with computerlike precision without killing the engine. Or without killing any well-meaning citizen who might have had the misfortune of being behind me on the hill! When it was all over, my head was spinning, my pulse was weak and, to be blunt, my bladder was full! In spite of all that, I learned something on that hill that many people don't learn about themselves and the things they hold on to. I learned when to let go!

When you come into the presence of God and His anointing, cast down your crowns and bend your knees. You can let it go and still not lose it. Like the 24 elders in Revelation, you must learn to trade a monument for a moment. The real reward you need to seek can be paid only by the one who hired you—God Himself. You see, the 24 elders knew that they had received results and rewards, but the real credit went to the Lord. They were wise enough not to be too impressed with their own success. They knew that it was God all the time. When you learn the time to take your foot off the clutch and give the glory back to God, you will be fulfilled in His presence and not frustrated by worshiping His presents!

I have a question I would like you to ponder. What makes a connoisseur of fine restaurants leave the elegant, aristocratic atmospheres and the succulent cuisine of gourmet food, only to stop by a hamburger joint for a sandwich and fries? Time's up. Here's the answer. Each of us has within us a need for balance and a sense of normalcy. It is so important that we balance our areas of expertise with plain everyday humanism. I shared in an earlier chapter how I started out preaching in the most adverse of circumstances. I don't think I really knew how adverse they were because I had nothing to compare them to. I went from sleeping in a child's bedroom of somebody's home to penthouse suites. I remember ministering in churches where the finances did not allow for a hotel room or even a real guest room. The evangelist would stay with the pastor, and usually the pastor had a house full of children. One of these bright-eyed children would have to give up his or her room to accommodate the man of God. I still pray for those families who gave what they had to make me as comfortable as they could. I earnestly appreciate it.

Imagine me, nearly six-foot-three-inches tall and the better part of 280 pounds, sleeping in a canopied bed designed for a ten-year-old girl with ribbons in her hair. I still break out into hysterical laughter as I picture myself sticking one extremity after the other out of the bed, trying to find a place to sleep! Now, I normally have excellent accommodations—though I admit that coming from my background, excellent accommodations can still mean a private room with a bed that can hold all my vital organs! God has blessed me to be able to minister in settings that can better accommodate the needs I have and support my family, which is a great blessing. In spite of all this improvement, on occasion I still seek to leave the well-insulated environment of a first-class establishment. I'll go find a little, "do drop in" kind of a place and then return to my suite with some down-home food and probably more grease than I could jog off in a year!

Balance helps to keep you from falling. It does not guarantee that you won't fall, but it does safeguard against the possibility. Never lose your balance—it will assist you in being a person and not just a personality. I believe that people need to see that God uses, as my friend Danniebelle wrote, "Ordinary People." If that weren't true, who would He use? Ordinary people who have extraordinary callings are the order of the day in this age. You will see in this age God raising Davids to the forefront, not Sauls. He will raise up men who don't look as if they would be kings. When you get your crown, don't use it to belittle people who need you. Instead cast it at the feet of the Lord who is the Giver of gifts as well as the preferred Prize of all that He gives.

Finally, the disciples asked the Lord to teach them how to pray. They had noticed that prayer was the helm that turned the ship toward the winds of destiny. They had noticed that Jesus periodically would disappear from the crowd. He would steal away and fill His arms with the presence of His Father embracing Him so He could affect the people and us later. They asked Him when they learned that the secret weapon of public success was just plain old prayer. It is not books, tapes, or videos; just groanings and moanings into the incense-filled altars of Heaven. Since Jesus had taught on everything else, they decided to ask Him to teach them how to pray.

And it came to pass, that, as He was praying in a certain place, when He ceased, one of His disciples said unto Him, Lord, teach us to pray, as John also taught his disciples (Luke 11:1).

After this manner therefore pray ye: Our Father which art in heaven, Hallowed be Thy name. Thy kingdom come. Thy will be done in earth, as it is in heaven. Give us this day our daily bread. And forgive us our debts, as we forgive our debtors. And lead us not into temptation, but deliver us from evil: For Thine is the kingdom, and the power, and the glory, for ever. Amen (Matthew 6:9-13).

When Jesus taught on prayer, He was teaching us how to steer the ship of life through the boisterous winds of adversity. If we can follow the "manner" of prayer, then we can follow the course of life. In order to pray effectively, we must know the personage of God. Hence He said, "Our Father." This establishes the basis of the relationship that we have with God. He is more than just Creator. He is our Father. We can create something and not be related to it, but if we father it, a part of us will always be in the things we father. So I must know that I am related to God and not just created by Him.

"Which art in heaven" addresses the fact that the God I am related to is the Ruler of the universe. He sits on the circle of the earth. The Bible teaches us that Heaven is

God's throne. So when we say, "which art in heaven," we are proclaiming the absolute sovereignty of our Father. We say, in effect, "Not only are You my Father, but You also are uniquely qualified to answer my prayer. You are related to me and empowered to perform." This phrase points directly to God's position. Now knowing the person and the position of Him, let us praise Him.

"I am not ashamed to praise You as I know the extent of Your authority. I take this time to approach You correctly. 'Hallowed be Thy name.' I almost forgot that just because You are my Father, my 'Abba,' that doesn't give me the right to show disrespect for Your position as Ruler in Heaven and earth. So 'hallowed be Thy name' reminds me that I must enter into Your gates with thanksgiving and into Your courts with praise." (See Psalm 100:4.) Praise will turn God's head. It will get His attention. I dare you to learn how to praise His name. When you praise His name, you are praising His character. He is "above board." He is holy!

When praises go up, blessings come down. So here comes the downpour of power. "Thy kingdom come" releases the downpour of the power of God. Praise will cause the very power of God to come down in your life. But what good is power without purpose? Thus Jesus taught the disciples, "Thy will be done in earth, as it is in heaven." That is a step up from power to purpose. Now the purpose of God comes down to your life. Have you ever gone through a time that God began to show you His purpose in your life? You can't have success without purpose!

"Give us this day our daily bread" deals with the provisions of Heaven coming down. This is more than a prayer; it is a divine direction. After receiving the power in your life, you come to understand the purpose. Never fear; if you know your purpose, God will release the provisions. Then the provisions you couldn't reach at one stage in your life suddenly fall like an early morning drizzle at another stage in your life.

There's nothing like provisions to give you the grace to forgive. It is easier to forgive when you discover that your enemies didn't stop the blessing from coming down. Here Jesus teaches His disciples to pray for the penitence of a forgiving heart. "Forgive us our debts, as we forgive our debtors." So penitence also is flowing down from the throne. Finally, Jesus taught us to seek deliverance from evil. Pray for the problems that still exist at every stage, and better still, at every success in life!

Having briefly examined the progression of the believer through this precious prayer, let us move on to the real point: the turning point. There must come in every person's life a turning point. Without it you can receive all of this power, purpose, provision, and penitence, overcome the problems, but still be burned out. God wants you to receive all of the great successes and accolades that He promised in His Word, but having received them, you must go beyond them to enter a level of understanding. None of this success is as important or as valuable as you initially thought. At this stage of life you begin to reevaluate what you call success. God gets the glory when He can give you anything and you can turn from all He gave you and still say from your heart, "Lord, I've found nothing as dear to me as You. My greatest treasure is the assurance of Your divine presence on my life. I am giving it all to You. 'For Thine is the kingdom,'—yes, I know I just prayed it down, but here it is. I am giving it back to You. Wait a minute, Lord. I want to say something else. 'And the power.' You can have that too. Oh, and about all that glory I've been getting—it's Yours as well! What? You want to know how long? Forever and ever and ever. It is so! Amen!"

Every other aspect of creation that receives anything, gives it back to God. The gold cornfields of the Midwest give back seed after the heavens send down the rains. The singing sound of the busy bee fills the air with the testimony of the pollen it has taken from the lilac and the rose, but gives back in the sweetness of the honey packed tightly in the comb. All the lesser kingdoms give to a greater kingdom. The mineral kingdom gives strength to the vegetable kingdom. The vegetable kingdom is consumed by the animal kingdom. Everything reaches the point of return. How strong can an apple tree grow without reaching the point where it needs to give apples back to the ground it grew from? Jesus cursed the fig tree because it had soaked up His water and flourished in His sun and yet, after all those blessings, had failed to reach the point of giving back one fig.

Near my home, crouched in the valley beneath the proud swelling mountains of West Virginia, runs a river whose rushing waters cannot be contained. The Elk River cannot keep receiving the cascading streams of water from the ground in the mountains without finally pushing its blessing on into the Kanawha River. This river, though larger, is no less able to break the laws of the kingdom. It drinks in the waters from its sources and then turns its attention to its destiny and gives back its waters to the system. So the mighty Ohio says Amen. From the Ohio to the Mississippi and on into the Gulf of Mexico, each body of water receives only to give. You see, my friend, success is not success without a successor.

We as Christians reach fulfillment when we come to the point where we bring to the Lord all that we have and worship Him on the other side of accomplishment. This need to return an answer to the Sender is as instinctive as answering a ringing telephone. There is a ringing in the heart of a believer that requires an answer. Why do we answer a phone? We do so because of our insatiable curiosity to know who is calling. He is calling us. His ring has sounded through our triumphs and conquests. A deep sound in the recesses of a heart turned toward God suggests that there is a deeper relationship on the other side of the blessing. As wonderful as it is to be blessed with promises, there is still a faint ringing that suggests the Blesser is better than the blessing. It is a ringing that many people overlook. The noise of the bustling, blaring sound of survival can be deafening. There must be a degree of spirituality in order to hear and respond to the inner ringing of the call of God!

He that hath an ear, let him hear what the Spirit saith unto the churches (Revelation 2:29).

I can think of no better illustration of this concept than the ten lepers in the Bible (see Luke 17:11-19). These ten distraught, grossly afflicted men were entombed by the prison of their own limitations. No matter who they were before, now they were lepers. Like bad apples, they were separated and cast out from friends and family. They were denied the feeling of warmth, love, and intimacy. Like all alienated groups, their only refuge was in each other's company. Pain brings together strange bedfellows. Ten men huddled together on the side of the road heard that Jesus was passing by. The most frightening thing that could happen in any hurting person's life is for Jesus to just pass by. These men, however, seized the moment. They took a risk...they cried out to Him. Desperate people do desperate things. Have you ever had a moment in your life that pushed you into a radical decision? These lepers cried out!

No one can hear like the Lord does. He can hear your thoughts afar off (see Ps. 139:2), so you know He can hear the desperate cry of someone who has nothing left to lose. When the ten cried, He responded. There were no sparks, no lightning, and no thunder, but the power of His words whisked them off into the realm of miracles. He told them to go show themselves to the priest. Thus they walked toward a goal. Step by step they walked. I don't know which dusty step it was along the way that brought to them a cleansing of their leprous condition. Perhaps, as with most people, it is no one step that brings you to success, but a relentless plowing through of obstacles and insecurities that brings the result of prayers answered and miracles realized.

Nevertheless, somewhere between Jesus' words and their going to the priest, they stepped into the greatest experience of their lives. Where there had been white, oozing, encrusted flesh, there was new skin as clear as a baby's. That is the wonderful thing about knowing Jesus— He takes away the old ugly scars of sin and leaves newness and fresh beginnings. Ten men walked like hikers on the side of the road with nothing but a word from God. They were changed while in the process of obeying the command of a Savior whom they had called out to a few miles back on the dusty road where all miracles are walked out. Peeking beneath their clothes, checking spots that had once been afflicted, they laughed in the wind as the reality of their deliverance became even more real with every step they took. There is no success like the success of a man who had to persevere in order to receive it. People appreciate the victory when they have to walk it out.

Beneath the clutter of their weary footsteps, God performed a miracle. Their healing meant much more than just a physical healing of leprosy. When Jesus healed them, He gave them back their dignity. He restored their potential to marry. He gave them back to their community. Thus success affects every area of life. Ten men giggling like children pulled at their clothes, gleefully showing each other their newly restored flesh. They had so much to do, so much to plan. The day seemed better and the sun much brighter. They probably floated over the road. But one man grew silent as his mind drifted beyond his own personal glee. For him there was something missing. It wasn't that he lacked appreciation for his healing; it was just a nagging feeling that this great moment was somehow incomplete. He had been told to go show himself to the priest. But perhaps the real priest was not in front of him, but behind him.

As his nine friends laughed and celebrated their victory, he began to lag behind. In the shadows of his mind lurked the figure of the Man on the road who spoke that word of healing. Why was he so discontented with what the other men seemed to be satisfied? After all, had not the Man sent them on their way? He pivoted on his heels like a soldier who had heard a command. He had an impulse, a pulling toward something beyond personal allurement. He decided to return to the Sender. The Sender seemed to be satisfied, but it was the former leper who wanted something more. He traveled back to the Sender, Jesus, the Miracle Worker. When he came to Jesus, he fell down at His feet and worshiped Him. Then Jesus asked a question. It's seldom that Jesus, the omniscient One, would ask anything—but this time He had a question. I shall never forget the pointedness of His question. He asked the one who returned, "Where are the nine?"

> *Every good gift and every perfect gift is from above, and cometh down from the Father of lights, with whom is no variableness, neither shadow of turning* (James 1:17).

Perhaps you are the one in ten who has the discernment to know that this blessing is nothing without the One who caused it all to happen. Most people are so concerned about their immediate needs that they fail to take the powerful experience that comes from a continued relationship with God! This is for the person who goes back to the

Sender of gifts with the power of praise. Ten men were healed, but to the one who returned Jesus added the privilege of being whole. Many will climb the corporate ladder. Some will claim the accolades of this world. But soon all will realize that success, even with all its glamour, cannot heal a parched soul that needs the refreshment of a change of peace. Nothing can bring wholeness like the presence of a God who lingers on the road where He first blessed you to see if there is anything in you that would return you from the temporal to embrace the eternal.

Remember, healing can be found anywhere, but wholeness is achieved only when you go back to the Sender with all of your heart and thank Him for the miracle of a second chance. Whatever you do, don't forget your roots. When you can't go anywhere else, my friend, remember you can go home!

Chapter 12

It's Just Your Time

Do you remember how in winter icicles hang from the roofs of old houses, pointing toward the ground like stalactites in a cave? As the cold blitz of winter was challenged by budding trees and warmer days, the icicles began to drip and diminish. Slowly the earth changed its clothes for a new season. I can plainly remember how as a child I felt the joys of each season. We packed away our sleds as spring came. We traded our coats for sweaters and then discarded them for just shirt sleeves as the sun liberated us from our wintry cocoons. In the silence of the night the sap that had hidden in the bottom of the trees moved upwards like a sluggish elevator making its ascent to the top. In the morning light buds turned to blossoms and by summer the blossoms showed their fruit.

Winter is just the prelude God plays to introduce the concerto of summer. In spite of its cold, frostbitten hand seizing our forest, lawns, and streams, its grip can still be broken through the patient perseverance of the season that is sensitive to timing and divine purpose. There is nothing like a sense of time. It cannot be faked. It is like seeing a choir sway to the beat of a gospel ballad. Someone invariably will be moving spastically, trying desperately to simulate a sense of timing. Moving his feet with all the grace of the Tin Man in *The Wizard of Oz*, he can't quite learn what the body has to sense. The lack of timing is as detrimental as planting corn in the bitter winds of an Alaskan winter. There may be absolutely nothing wrong with the seed or the ground, just the time in which the farmer chose to expect the process to occur.

Assuming that you now understand the necessity of small beginnings, and assuming that you realize whatever you have will not replace the One who gave it and that success only creates a platform for responsibility to be enlarged—then you can begin to ascertain where you are on the calendar, the divine almanac of God. Did you know that God has an almanac? Perhaps you do not know what an almanac is. My mother always consulted the almanac to determine the best time to plant the crop she intended to harvest. It is a calendar that presents the seasons and cycles of a year. You see, the principle of seed time and harvest will not override the understanding of time and purpose. God does everything according to His eternal almanac of time and purpose!

In autumn, you turn over the ground so last year's stalks and stems can become next year's harvest. Broken clods freshly turned, filled with crushed cornstalks and covered with manure, form the mulch you need to prepare the ground and replenish the starving soil after the previous yield. Like the ground that has given much and received little, you too need to be broken and turned over, allowed to rest for a time, and prepared for the next season of yield. Perhaps you have just completed a time of being turned over and undergoing manure-filled experiences. That period was just a prerequisite for a miracle! Thank God for the seasons of rest He gives to His children. If the ground produced without ever resting, it would soon be stripped of all the precious minerals it needs to be productive.

> For if thou altogether holdest thy peace at this time, then shall there enlargement and deliverance arise to the Jews from another place; but thou and thy father's house shall be destroyed: and who knoweth whether thou art come to the kingdom for such a time as this? (Esther 4:14)

Mordecai taught Queen Esther an essential lesson when he spoke those words. He wanted her to realize that God had given her an opportunity to be a blessing. Now, it wasn't given to her so she could brag about the nobility of which she became a part. God isn't interested in human grandeur. When He allows us to ascend into the clouds, it is only so we can stop the rain with the enlightenment we gained from the laborious progression of our own experiences. Mordecai showed Esther that God had been grooming her all her life for this moment. In spite of the tremendous challenge set before her, she was the woman for the job. She was God's choice, a handmaiden fitly chosen and wonderfully endowed for the acquisition of a victorious report.

> *Go, gather together all the Jews that are present in Shushan, and fast ye for me, and neither eat nor drink three days, night or day: I also and my maidens will fast likewise; and so will I go in unto the king, which is not according to the law: and if I perish, I perish* (Esther 4:16).

Mordecai's counsel prepared Esther's mind for the purpose God had from the beginning for elevating her position. Counsel may prepare your mind, but only fervent prayer can prepare your spirit for the vast undertakings that come with it being your time. No one counsel will prepare your heart like prayer.

I once met an evangelist at a retreat in Chicago. He woke every morning while the rest of the ministers were still asleep and went jogging for hours in the early morning dew. When I awoke, he was coming down the hall with a flushed face and glistening with perspiration. He was smiling like he knew a secret. I asked him later, "Why don't you try to rest instead of racing around the grounds like you are preparing for a fight with Muhammad Ali?" He laughed, and I will never forget his answer. He said, "Every day I read for my mind. I pray for my spirit. And I run for my body." He explained, "If I touch all three areas, all parts of my being have been exercised to perform well." I looked down at my bountiful waist and thought, "Two out of three isn't bad."

Esther was a wise woman; she called a fast. Once Mordecai had exercised her mind through wise counsel, she called a time of fasting and prayer to prepare her spirit. She knew that prayer undergirds the spirit and keeps a person from sagging beneath the weight of opposition. Not only did she pray, but she also taught everyone under her authority to pray as well. I have learned that it is difficult to work with people who do not pray. Even our children pray. Now, I'm not suggesting that we are perfect. We don't pray because we are perfect—we pray because we are not! Prayer is a strong defense against satanic attack. If Esther had not prayed, she would have fallen prey to the cunning devices of Haman, her wicked enemy!

> *Now it came to pass on the third day, that Esther put on her royal apparel, and stood in the inner court of the king's house, over against the king's house: and the king sat upon his royal throne in the royal house, over against the gate of the house. And it was so, when the king saw Esther the queen standing in the court, that she obtained favour in his sight: and the king held out to Esther the golden sceptre that was in his hand. So Esther drew near, and touched the top of the sceptre* (Esther 5:1-2).

Esther's changing her apparel signifies our need to alter our circumstances to facilitate the success of the vision that is before us. Everything must be committed to the goal—body, soul, and spirit. When the king beheld a prepared person, he granted an expected end. He drew her into his presence because she had prepared herself for her time. Please hear me; there is a blessing on the horizon for the person of purpose. Only the prepared will be eligible to receive this endowment from the Lord, so be ready!

Like sands cascading down in an hourglass, time silently slips away, without the chance of retrieval, from

almost everyone everyday. The misuse of anything as precious as time should be a crime. If someone steals your car,
it would be an inconvenience but not a tragedy because
you can easily acquire another. If someone snatches your
wallet, it would be an annoyance but a few phone calls
would salvage the majority of your concerns. But who can
you call if you suffer the loss of time—and not just time,
but *your time*? Who can afford to miss their time? I can't,
can you?

Ask God to give you the patience you need to become
empowered to perform. You may feel like a child waiting
in line at a carnival. There will always be times when other
people receive their dues and you are forced to wait your
turn. This is not injustice; it is order. There is nothing
unjust about order. But after I have waited my turn and
paid my dues, there comes a time when it is all mine. The
most frightening thing I can think of is the possibility of
missing my time. Generally, somewhere on the other side
of a tremendous test is the harvest of your dream. If you
have planted the seeds of a promise and watered them
thoroughly with the tears of struggle, then this is your
time. Woe unto the person who has seeds without water.
The tears of struggle become the irrigation of the Holy
Spirit. It is through your own tear-filled struggles that God
directs the waters of life to the field of your dreams.

They that sow in tears shall reap in joy (Psalm 126:5).

Greatness has a tremendous thirst. This thirst is
quenched in the tear-stained struggle toward destiny. One
thing I learned about life is neither fellowship nor friendship can lower the price of personal sacrifice. What I mean

is, no one can water your dreams but you. No matter how many people hold your hand, you still must shed your own tears. Others can cry with you, but they can't cry for you! That's the bad news. The good news is there will be a harvest at the end of your tears!

On the other hand, you must know when you have shed enough tears. It is important that you don't get stuck in a state of lamentation. In short, don't overwater the promise! A certain amount of tears is necessary during the time of sowing. But when you have come into harvest, don't let the devil keep you weeping. Tears are for the sower, but joy is for the harvester. Harvest your field with joy. You've paid your dues and shed your tears—now reap your benefits. It's your turn. Reap in knee-slapping, teeth-baring, hand-clapping, foot-stomping joy!

He that goeth forth and weepeth, bearing precious seed, shall doubtless come again with rejoicing, bringing his sheaves with him (Psalm 126:6).

Everything has a season and a purpose (see Eccles. 3:1). You need to understand that God is just and that He appropriates opportunities to advance according to His purpose. I don't know whether this is true for everyone, but usually obscurity precedes notoriety. The first Psalm teaches that the blessed man meditates on the Word while he waits. It says that you bring forth fruit in your own season. It is good to recognize your season and prepare for it before it comes. But the fruit will not grow prior to its right season. Don't demand fruit when it is not in season. Even restaurant menus have a notation that says certain items can be served only when their fruit is in season.

> *And he shall be like a tree planted by the rivers of water, that bringeth forth his fruit in his season; his leaf also shall not wither; and whatsoever he doeth shall prosper* (Psalm 1:3).

I call those seasons "green light" time. You feel as though you have been waiting without seeing any results, almost like a car waiting at an intersection. Then the light suddenly changes from red to green and you are free to move. When God changes the light in your life from red to green, you can accomplish things that you tried to do at other times but could not perform. What an exciting time it is to suddenly find your engine kicking into gear and your turbines turning in harmonious production. Your tires screech from a dead stop to jet speed in seconds and bang! You are on the road again.

This is an exciting time for the prepared believer. I believe with all my heart that soon people whom God had waiting their turn will burst to the forefront and pull into the fast lane. Trained by patience and humbled by personal challenges, they will usher in a new season in the cycle of the Kingdom. Are you a part of what God is doing, or are you still looking back at what God has done? I want to see you burn some spiritual rubber for Jesus!

There may be some degree of reservation in the mind of the thinking person. "What if I enter my season and experience the rich blessings God has been promising for a long time, and then the season ends? How can I stand to go back into seclusion and be content? Isn't it difficult, once a person has been a main player, to become subdued and lethargic after being exposed to the racing, titillating feeling of a green light time in life?" All of these are excellent questions, ones that must be addressed. After all, what good is having your season if over your head gather the gloomy clouds of warning that keep thundering a nagging threat in your ears? They threaten that all you are doing now will not last.

First, let me rebuke the spirit of fear. Fear will hide in the closet as we are blessed and make strange noises when no one else is around. We need to declare God to this fear. We dare not fall in love with what God is doing, but we must always be in love with who God is. God does not change. That's why we must set our affections on things that are eternal. He said, "For I am the Lord, I change not" (Mal. 3:6a). It is such a comfort, when the chilly voice of fear speaks, to know that God doesn't change. His purpose doesn't change. His methods may change, but His ultimate purpose doesn't. People have a need to know what comes next. God doesn't always make us privy to such information, but He has promised that if we walk uprightly, He will not withhold any good thing from us (see Ps. 84:11). I therefore conclude that if God withheld it, then it was no longer working for my good. I am then ready for the next assignment—it will be good for me.

The thing we must always remember is God can bless us in many different areas. Even while we were in the waiting periods of our lives, some other area was being blessed. There are really no "down" times in God. We only feel down when, like spoiled children, we demand that He continue to give us what He did at one stage without appreciating the fact that we are moving from one stage to another. It is what the Word calls going from faith to faith (see Rom. 1:17).

God has put too much training into you to leave you without any area of productivity. He has been grooming you in the furnace of affliction. When He begins to move you into your season, don't allow even well-meaning people to intimidate you with the fear of change.

When I was a young man who had recently accepted Christ in a real and personal way, there was an elderly lady in our church who used to sing a song that said something like this: "Anyway You bless me, Lord, I'll be satisfied." What a wonderful place to be in—a place where you can trust the God whom you have believed upon to operate for your ultimate good. He knows how much and how long to raise the crop in your field. There is a peace that Christians must have in order to enjoy life. I believe one of Saul's greatest mistakes was to fall in love with the kingdom and not the King! He was so intimidated when God decided to move someone into his position that he tried to kill his successor. You would be surprised how many good people try to kill their successors. Mothers are jealous of their own daughters. Fathers belittle their own sons. If your time as a good boxer is up, then why can't you learn the art of being an excellent coach? You see, there always is an area where you can be fruitful; it simply may not be the same area all the time.

> *Preach the Word; be prepared in season and out of season; correct, rebuke and encourage—with great patience and careful instruction* (2 Timothy 4:2 NIV).

Speaking of coaches, the apostle Paul, who was an excellent minister of the gospel, began in the winter of his ministry to pour his knowledge into his successor. He wasn't jealous. He began the process of coaching the greatness that he recognized in the life of another man. Here he releases a concept that is very powerful. He counsels Timothy to develop the ability to be prepared in season and out of season. It seems almost conflicting to suggest that God wants us to be prepared in season as well as when our season seems to be receding. I could never quite understand this verse until another preacher began to share with me some farming techniques that I had not applied to this pursuit of excellence in ministry or in any other area.

The farmer who continuously produces crops can do so because he produces more than one type of crop. He has several different fields and he rotates a certain crop from one field to another. He plants corn in one field and it grows and produces ears of yellow corn on tall green stalks that sway in the wind and gleam in the sun. Eventually the corn goes out of season. The farmer takes the old stalks that turned brown and withered and plows them under. Now, a farmer always thinks in terms of tomorrow. He plows and fertilizes the field and allows it to rest from growing corn. Meanwhile in the other field the alfalfa is cut for the last crop of hay and it too is plowed. In the spring the farmer rotates his crops; the field that once grew corn now produces alfalfa, and the field that previously was planted in alfalfa now sprouts cornstalks. This coverall-clad soldier will always be productive because he understands the importance of being multifaceted.

Paul tells Timothy to be instant in season and out of season. He then tells him to be diverse. According to his instructions, we must reprove and rebuke. We also must be able to let things rest and encourage others. I believe many people lose their sense of self-worth because they fail to diversify themselves. Then, when the season of one gift is over, they are unprepared for any other area. If we listen carefully to the voice of God, we can be productive at every stage of life. It doesn't matter whether we are respected as players or as coaches. What matters is ultimately we contribute on some level to the game. We need to stay in the game. In short, diversity is a key to longevity.

Psalm 1 says that the blessed man doesn't just grow; he is also planted. Do you realize that God plants the feet of the blessed man? Never does he "just happen." He is not a weed. He is planted at a specific time in a specific place to accomplish a divine purpose. I have noticed that people who always move from place to place do not grow very well. The blessed man is planted! If you have been planted, you grow down before you grow up. I simply mean that God isn't concerned about how high your trunk grows. He is concerned about how deep your roots go. He knows that the real challenge is to produce quality, not quantity.

The Master has created a masterpiece in you. He has taken every struggle and test, every mishap and neglect, to cultivate in you the soil needed to make you reproductive. Contrary winds were sent to blow you away from people and cliques that would not create a climate conducive for what God wants to do in your life. In the light of His own divine "Sonshine," He has enlightened and established you. He is about to unveil a new realm of glory in your life.

What a celebration ought to be going on inside you at this moment. There ought to be a threefold celebration going on in your heart right now. First, you ought to look back over your times of obscurity, when He was plowing and fertilizing you, and thank God that you are still here to attest to His sustaining power. A lesser vessel would not have survived your testimony. Second, look around you at the blessings that you have right now. With a twinkle in your eye and a melody in your heart, thank God for what He is doing even at this moment. Your freshly cultivated ground is full of seeds and unborn potential. Who knows all that God has planted in you. He has begun a work—a good work—in you. Celebrate that every time you wake up in the morning. Look over your straw-covered fields, fan back the birds of doubt and fear, and thank God. Breathe the fresh air into grateful lungs, being glad just to be here.

Third, you should celebrate what God is about to do in your life. Your heart ought to be thumping in your chest; your blood ought to be racing like a car engine about to peel rubber! You are about to step into the greatest harvest of your life. The enemy knows you are about to be harvested. That's why he fought you like he did. He realizes that this is your time. Don't you? A powerful prophetic move is about to explode over your life. Are you ready for the word of the Lord that was spoken over you to come to pass? Get ready! Hurry, get your mind ready, change your clothes! Put on your shouting shoes! When the news that's in your spirit gets in your mind, tears of joy will wet the runway for your takeoff. Don't ever read about anyone else and wish you were him. Don't ever wish you had lived at any other time. You were created for this moment—and this moment was created for you! Stop reading and look at the clock. Laugh to yourself and praise your God. Do you know what time it is? *It's your time!*

Additional copies of this book and other
book titles from DESTINY IMAGE are
available at your local bookstore.

Call toll-free: 1-800-722-6774.

Send a request for a catalog to:

Destiny Image® Publishers, Inc.
P.O. Box 310
Shippensburg, PA 17257-0310

*"Speaking to the Purposes of God for This
Generation and for the Generations to Come."*

**For a complete list of our titles,
visit us at www.destinyimage.com.**